I0750715

For the people who take great care to remember their loved ones,
lost on the road but never forgotten,
and the reminder they offer the rest of us...

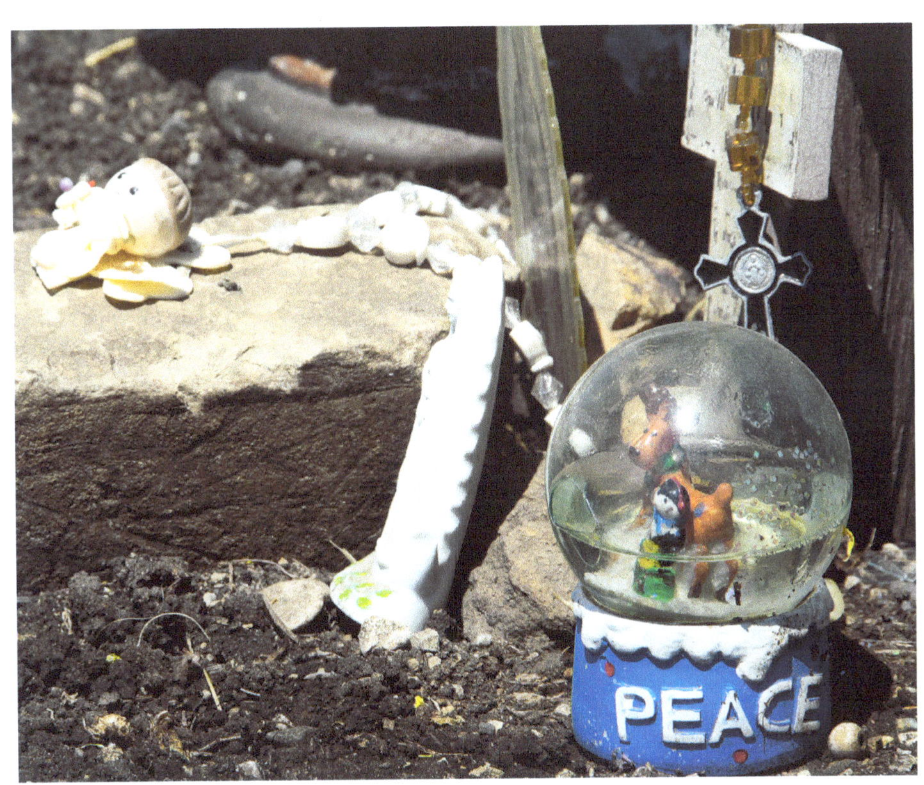

Las Cruces

Intersections

Robbie Kaye

FORWARD

As an author and educator at a small university near Portland, Oregon, I became acquainted with Robbie Kaye when she enrolled in "Making Waves with Words", an undergraduate writing class. One of the archetypes we studied is that of the pilgrim or wayfarer. Robbie's book, *Las Cruces*, illuminates this prevailing pattern of human behavior.

Throughout world literature, this pattern recurs, as seen in the book of *Exodus, Don Quixote, Pilgrim's Progress, Travels with Charley* and many other works. The motif of sojourner also distinguishes popular melodies, like *Sentimental Journey, Dust in the Wind, I'm Just a Rolling Stone*, to name just a few compelling examples.

Robbie Kaye's collection of photos invites the viewer to accompany contemporary residents and those who travel across borders, as they experience the power and poignance of the desert southwest landscape.

At a period in American history, when this terrain tests the stamina of sojourners and the patience of citizens, the imagery of *Las Cruces* serves to console, as well as to embody a sign of contradiction.

Joan Maiers

Lake Oswego, OR

"(D)escansos are symbols that mark a death. Right there, right on that spot, someone's journey in life halted unexpectedly. To make descansos means taking a look at your life and marking where the small deaths, *las muertes chicitas,* and the big deaths, *las muertes grandotas*, have taken place."

"*Women Who Run with the Wolves*," Clarissa Pinkola Estes

Life was shifting for me in that year, 2001. I'd suspended pursuing music after twenty plus years in that career. I'd taken a leave of absence from my job at UCSC. I was driving across the country alone except for my sweet dog, "Shooby", en route from California to a writing fellowship in Vermont.

Driving through Bryce Canyon was spectacular. The red rock perched high beneath a deep blue sky, sprinkled with snow was breathtaking. Being a city girl, I had never seen this kind of landscape in winter.

I left that canyon in awe and as I was driving on the highway I passed a large white cross standing on the hill of the median. In big black letters it read, "Saturday Warrior."

I don't know if it was the canyon or just driving that opened up my senses, but as I passed this particular cross, I felt extremely drawn to it.

I continued on the highway for several miles and then a feeling came over me. The intrigue was too strong and I knew I had to go back for this hauntingly beautiful marking.

I pulled off, turned around and drove back to the cross.

So many questions ran through my mind: who did this cross belong to? Why was it there? What is the story?

At that time, I was not pursuing a career in photography but but still felt compelled to take that photograph of *Saturday Warrior*...and then the next cross...and the next.

I found roadside crosses in New Mexico, Arizona and all over the country during my travels in the last 19 years.

I'd written many songs while driving in my car and whenever I drove long distances, I kept a notebook close by for journaling.

After seeing these crosses, Las Cruces, words poured out of me.
By the time I reached New York I had completed twenty-one poems of fictionalized voices coming from beneath the earth. Voices of death. Big death. I contemplated the small deaths I'd experienced by that time.

That trip was seventeen years ago. In my travels, I continue to notice crosses and photograph them. Each time I see another cross – in Hawaii, California, any roadside – I pause. Take note. Acknowledge. It's an occasion to ask myself: where am I in my life?

This sign of death calls to mind little deaths. The unexpected changes: the fragility of life.

I take a photograph in reverence.

Robbie Kaye

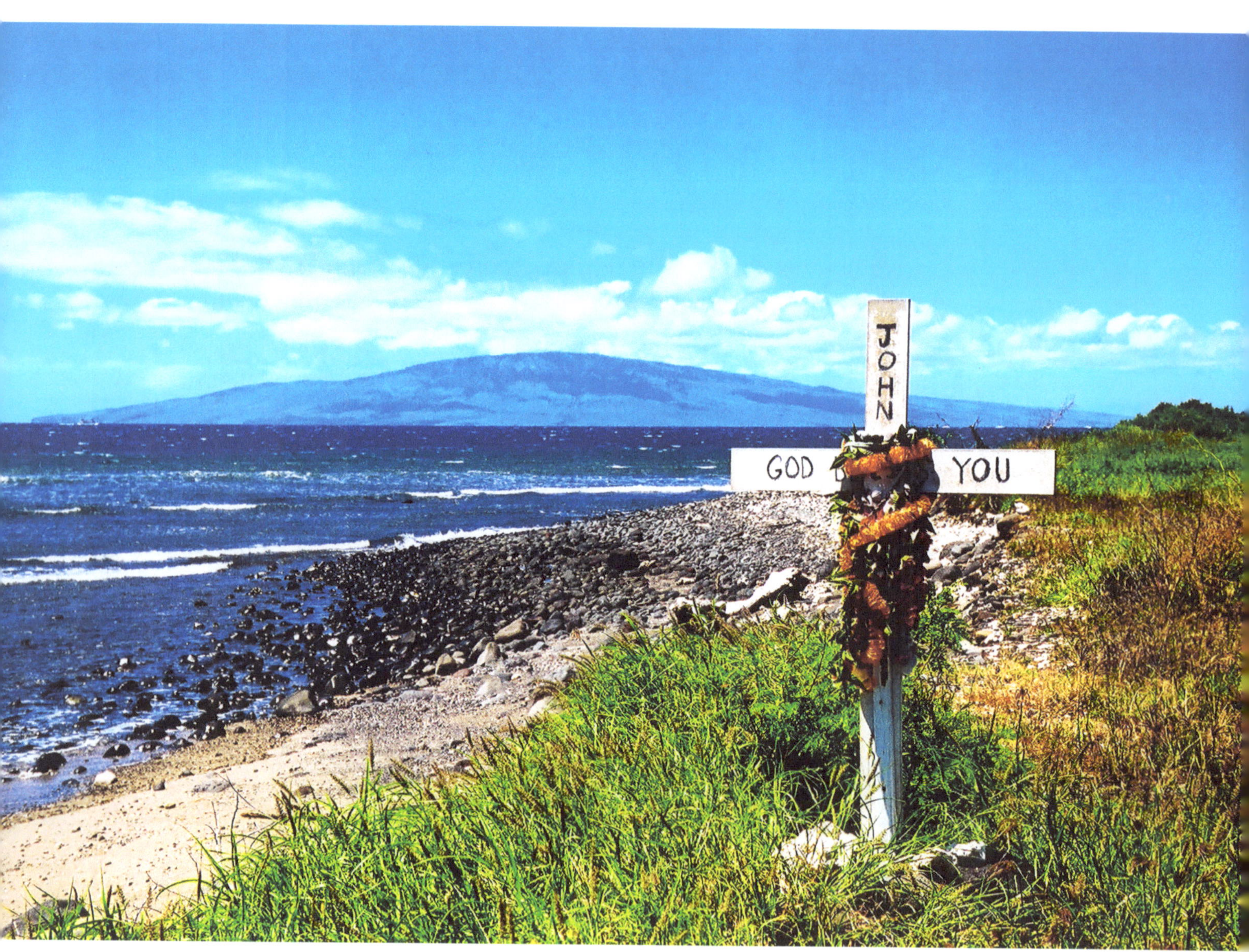

John, Hana, HI 2003

Serves You Right

'Serves you right'

You're thinking in the darkest corner of your heart

Intoxicated with hatred
Inebriated with rage

You want to kick my cross
Toss my wreath
Spit on my flowers
Cut my balloons
Curse my memory

I understand

I was not drunk

I understand

The woman who killed your son

Was

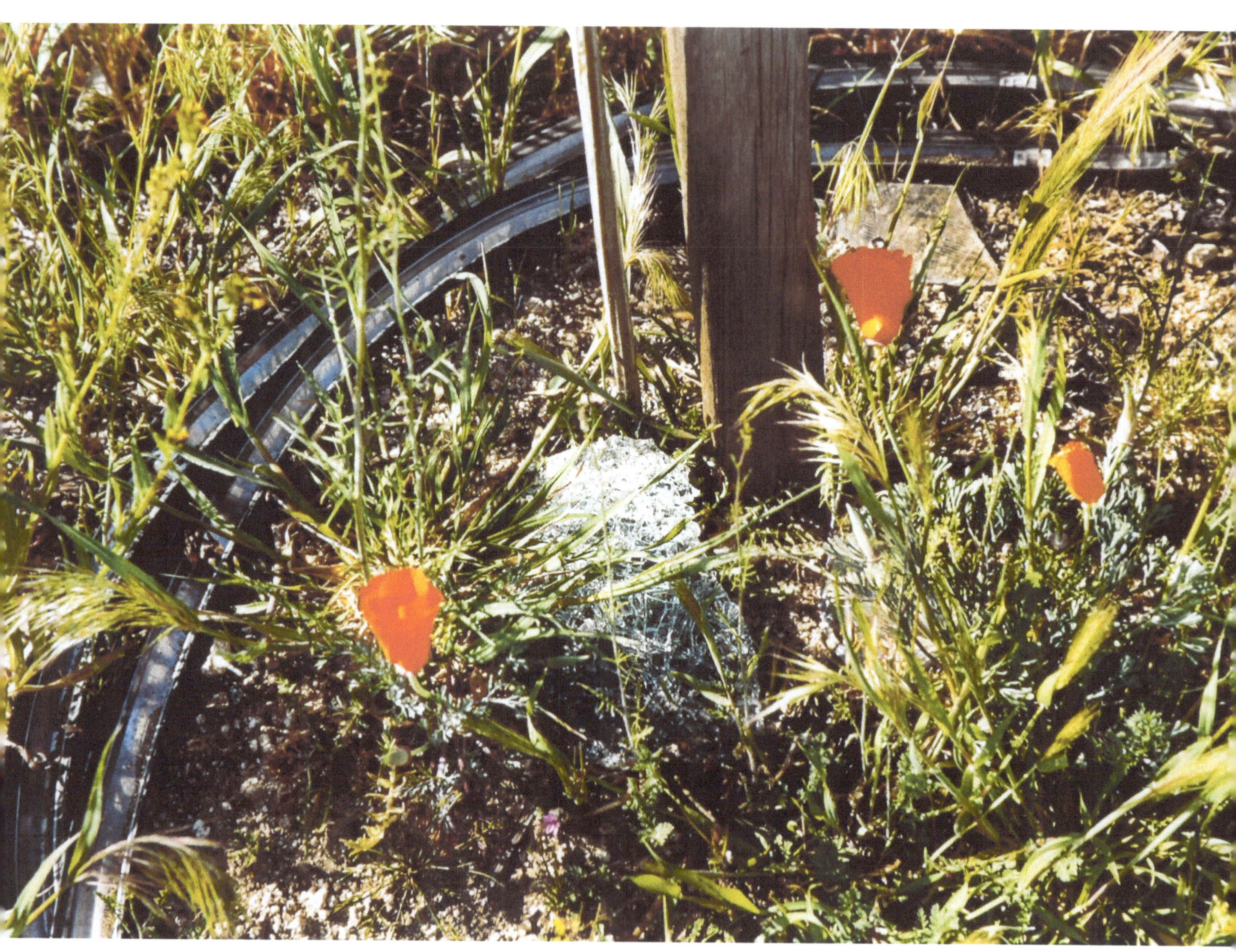

Wheel Spoke, Lancaster, CA 2006

The Wheel Spoke

From here, I watch my family drive by
My mother sends me a prayer
She makes the sign of the cross
That's her way of saying hello

She remembers my face
Small, young
A nickel's worth in years

I remain in her memory
Like rust on the handlebars of my purple stingray

It lies on the crabgrass
In the corner of our backyard

Once a playground
Now a cemetary

The mangled wheel
Half twisted spoke
Endures

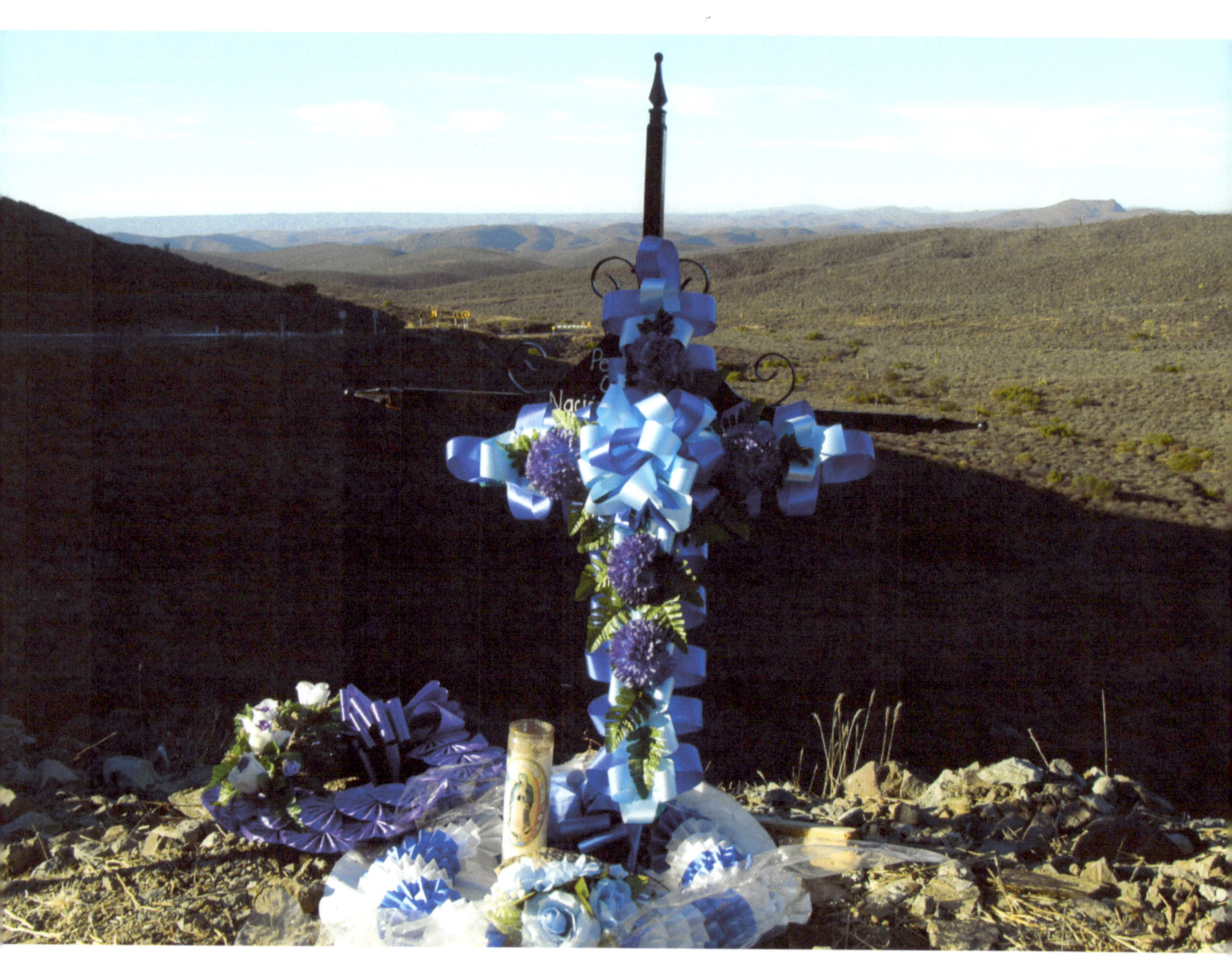

Blue in Baja, CA 2015

A Good Place To Die

This looks like a good place to die
Surrounded by canyons
Embraced by Mother Earth

She opens her arms
I fall into them

Like a baby, I am cradled and rocked
Seduced into long, deep sleep

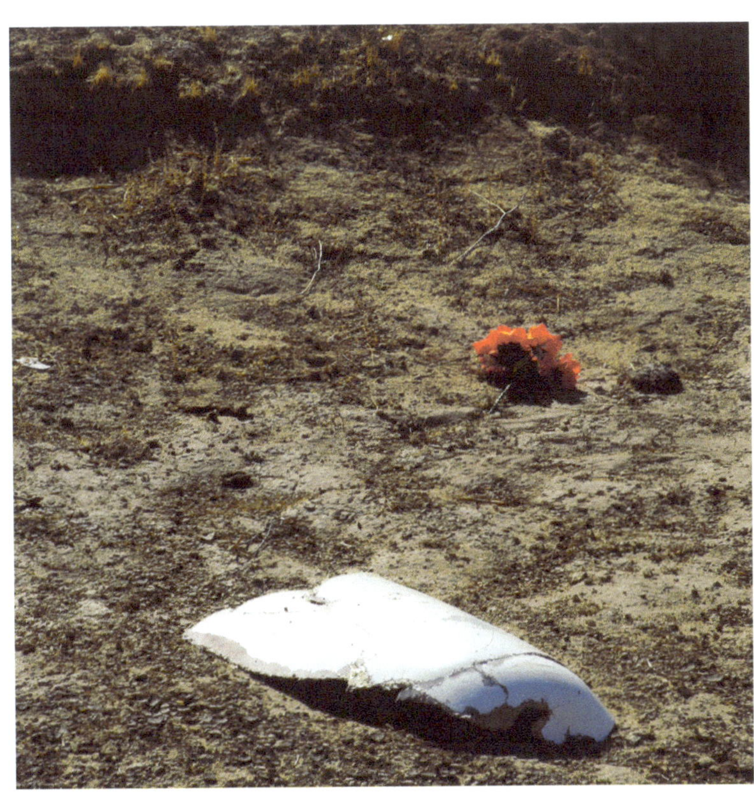

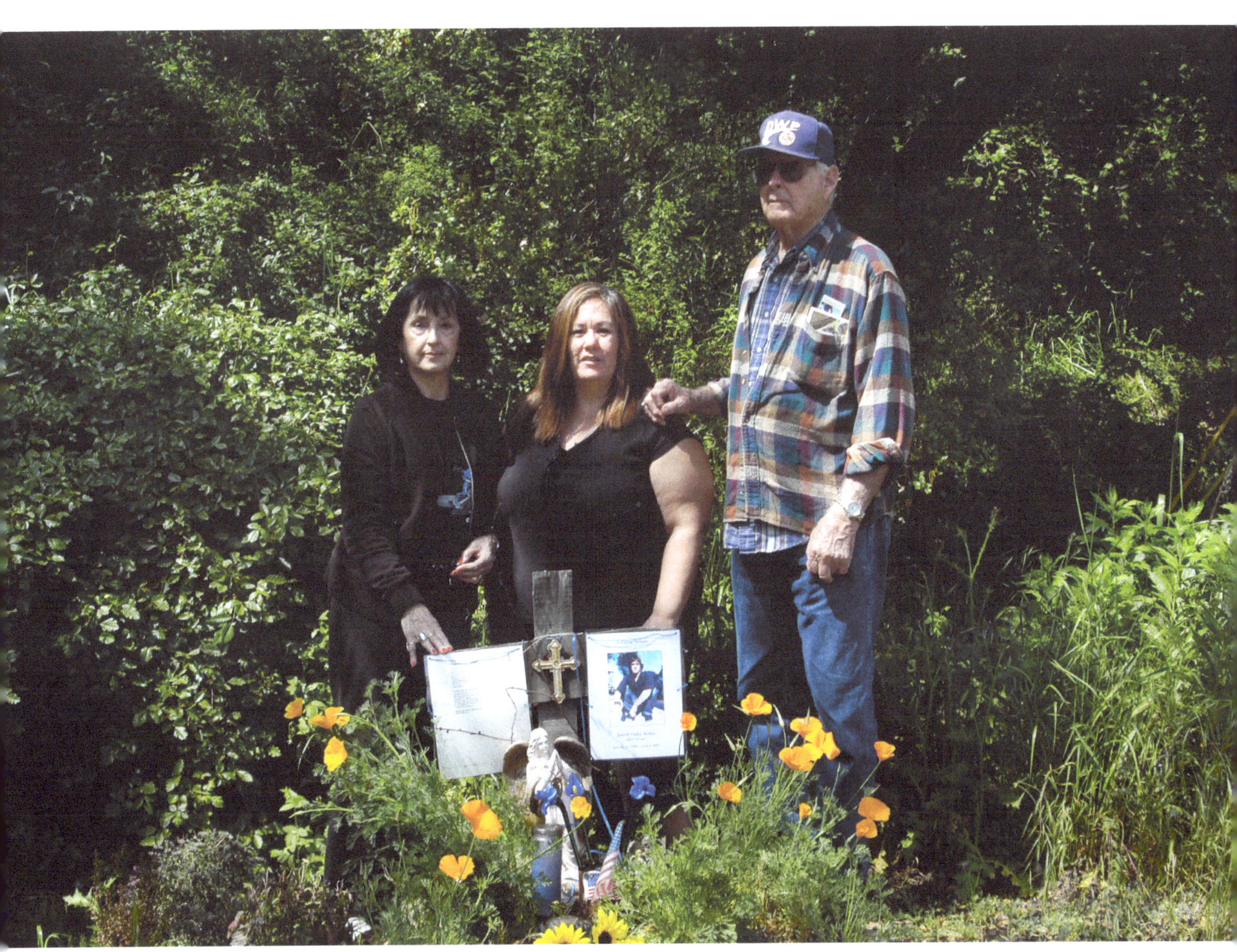

Dusty's mother, aunt and grandfather. Dusty was riding his motorcycle on Old Topanga Canyon Road. He was 23.

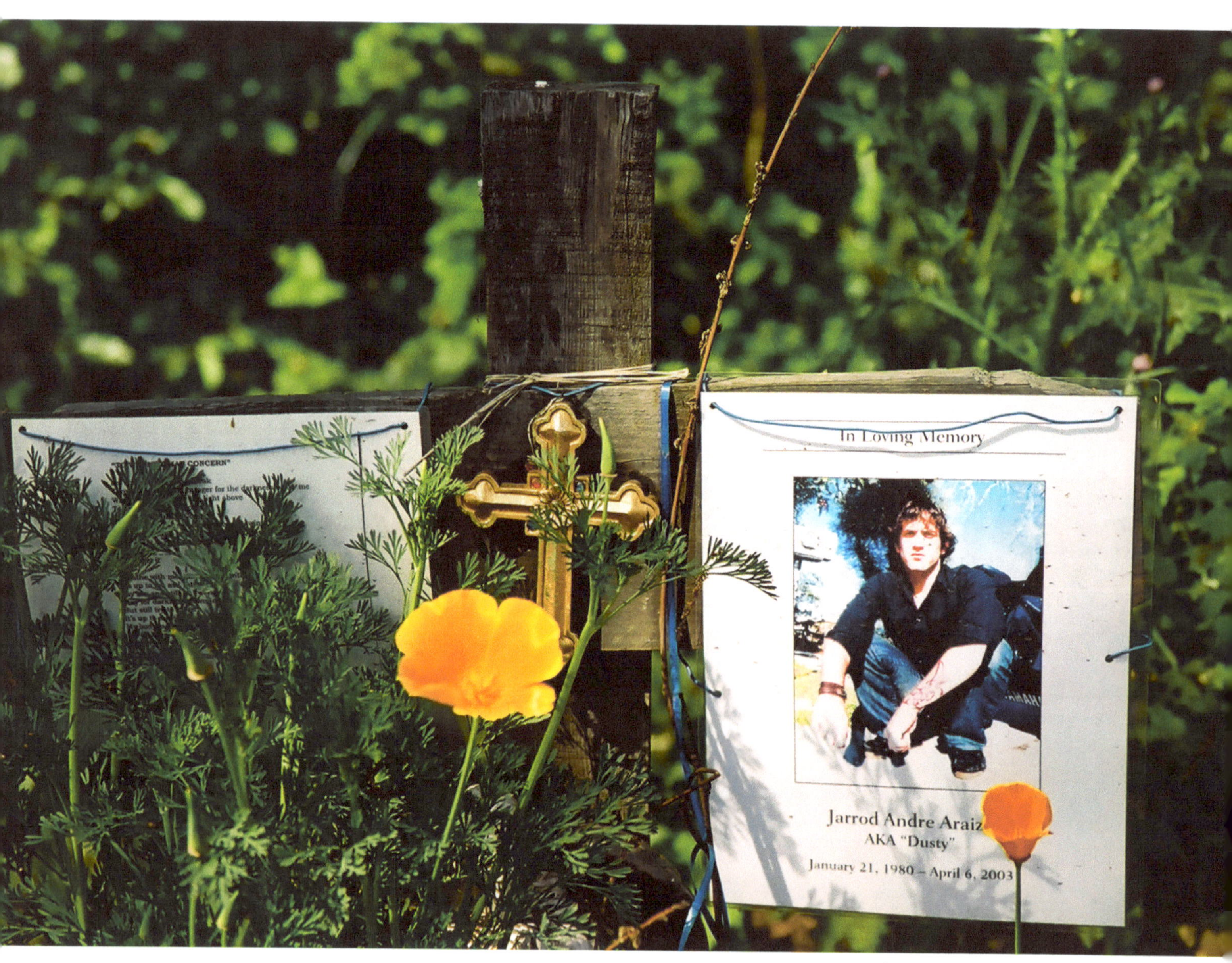

Dusty, Topanga, CA 2010

Don't Worry Mama

Don't cry mama, it aint so bad
Come a little closer, I can't see you

I know you don't like to come here much
You prefer the cemetary, the proper burial ground

But you know my soul is right here
This is where my spirit said goodbye to my body
And you know mama?
My spirit's been soaring ever since

That old tomb stone in the graveyard
Is so cold, so grey
It don't say nothing, nothing really about me mama

See mama?
Here, I got a football and a jersey with my number on it

Joey D. made that cross with oak
Polyurethaned it twelve times so it don't get ruined by the rain

So don't worry mama
I'm awright

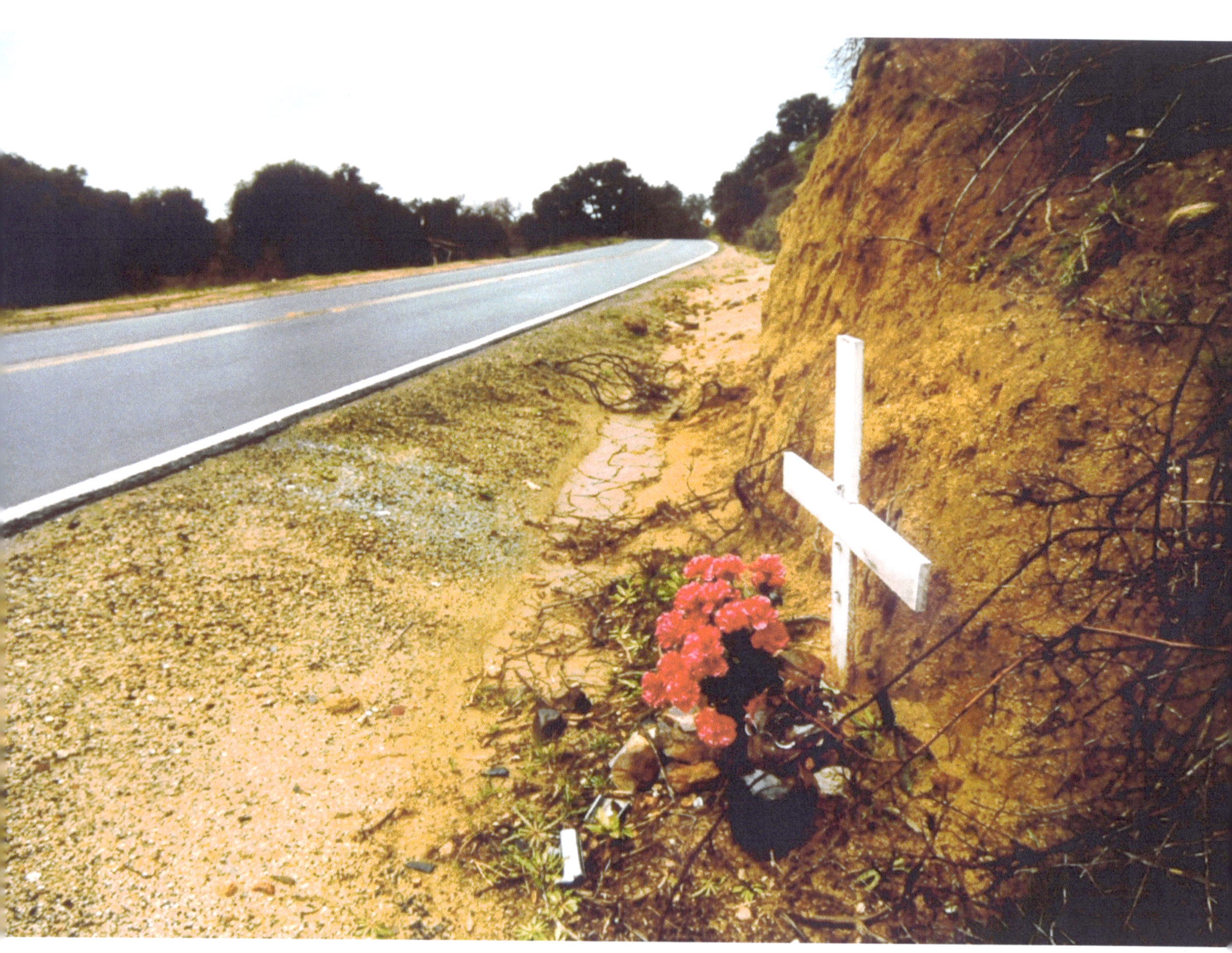

Warner Springs, CA 2008

My Love

If I could push my fingers through this cold, damp earth
I would reach for the soft skin on your face
I'd wipe that lonely tear, paving its way down your cheek
For the next…and the next…

My love
It was no fault of yours
Nor your punishment to be alive
But a gift
And now, it's time for you to move on as I have

It's only my body that is dead
My soul remembered, continues to thrive

I will be with you in all that you do, see and hear
You shall always have

My love

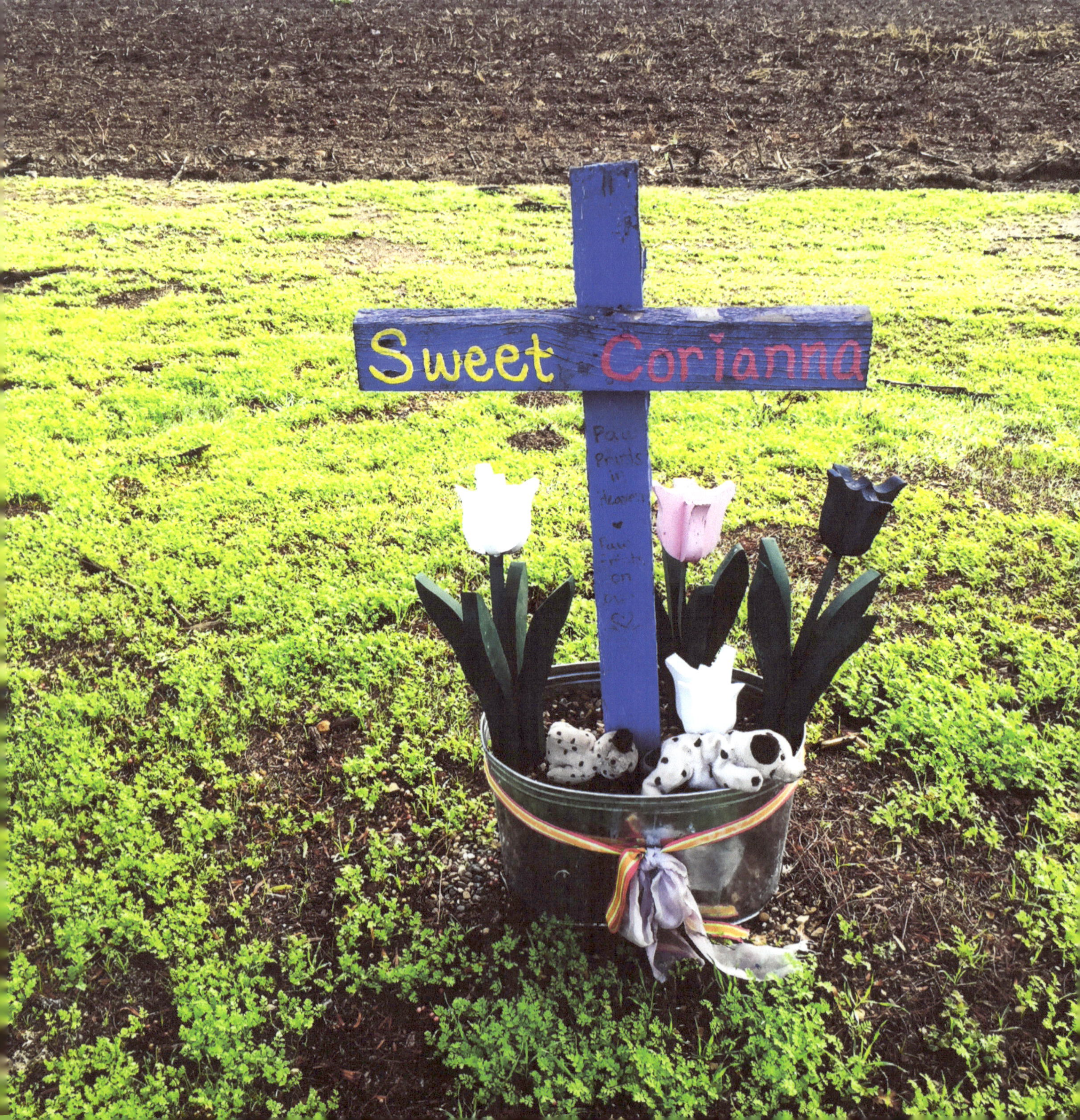
Sweet Corianna

Las Cruces Para Los Animales

I dedicate Las Cruces
To all the animals that lay dead on the side of the road

Deer, dog, cat, racoon, elk, possum, skunk
and all creatures

They do not get in our way
We get in their way, their land, their fields
Where we built winding roads and pathways for our convenience

Not many crosses for them

They are killed in their domain as they roam in innocence
Their life come to a brutal end

We, as trespassers can at least say a prayer
And plant a mindful thought in their memory

Let us say
Rest in Peace
Thank you
Good-bye
And

Forgive us

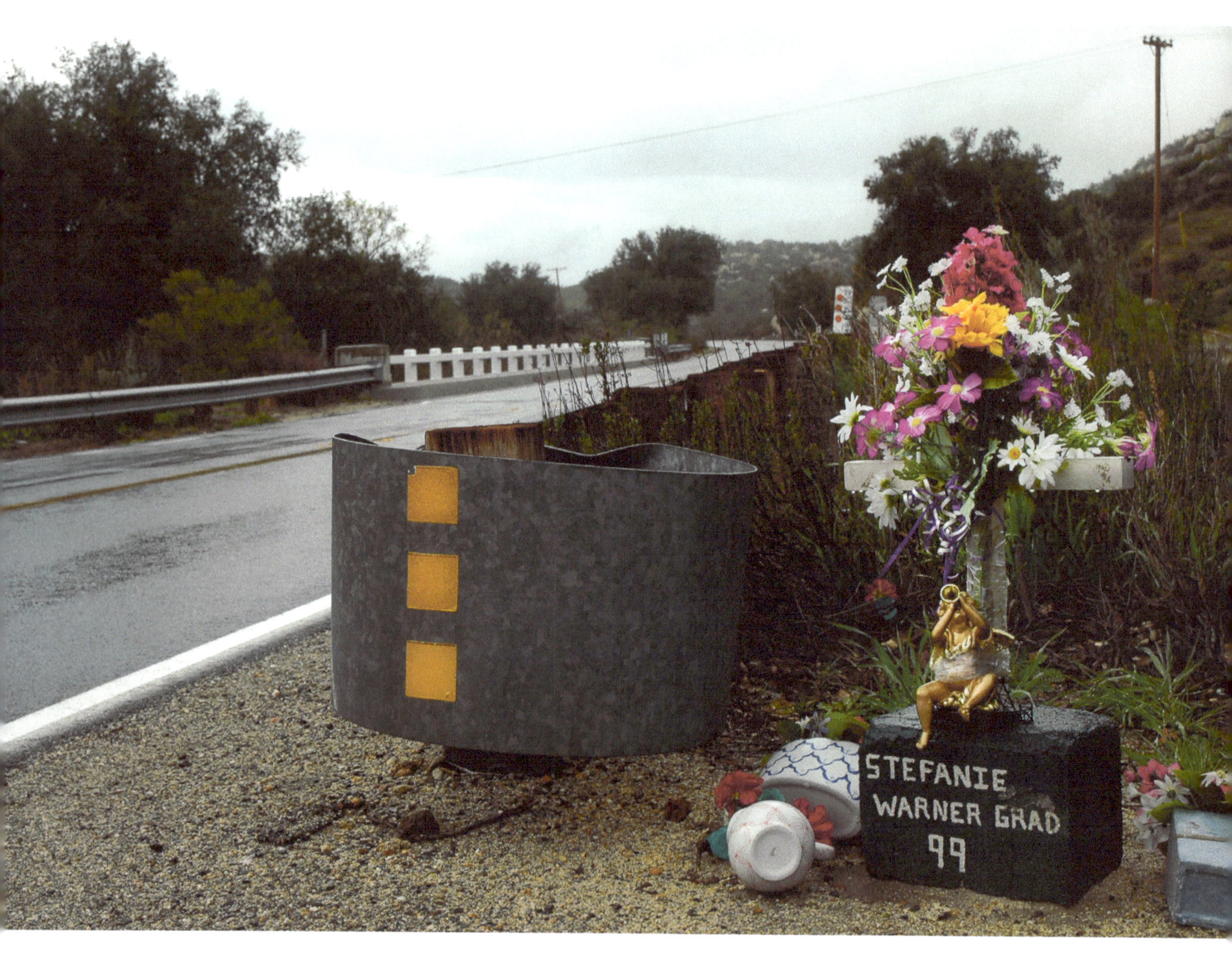

Stefanie, Warner Grad, Warner Springs, CA 2005

Thoughts In Passing

As you pass
I know you are wondering about me

How old?
How tall?
Married?
A parent?
A child?
A teacher?
A lover?
Did it happen fast?
Slow?
Was I drunk?
Stoned?
As you pass,
I am wondering
About you

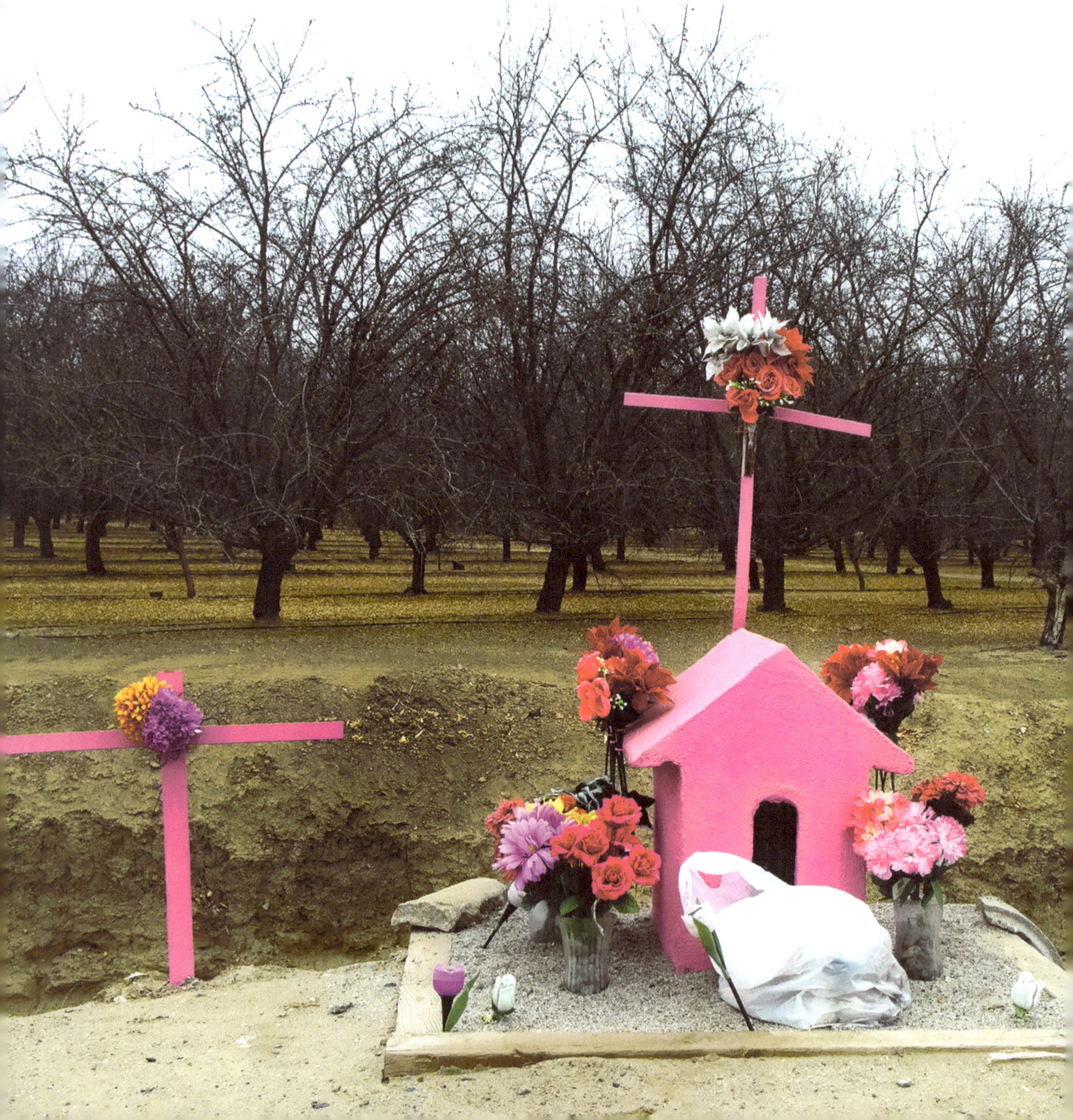

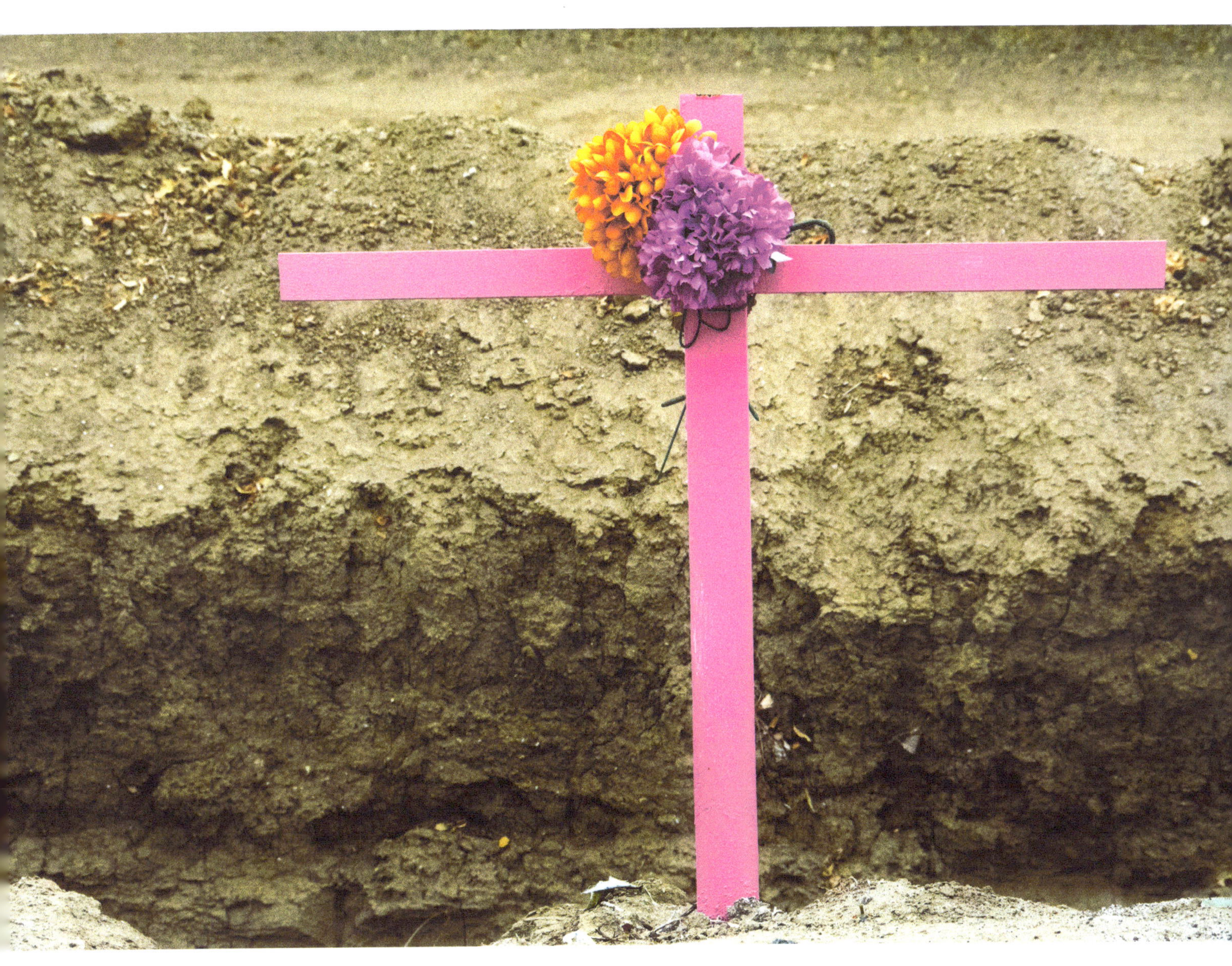

Pink Cross
Old River Road, Bakersfield, CA 2018

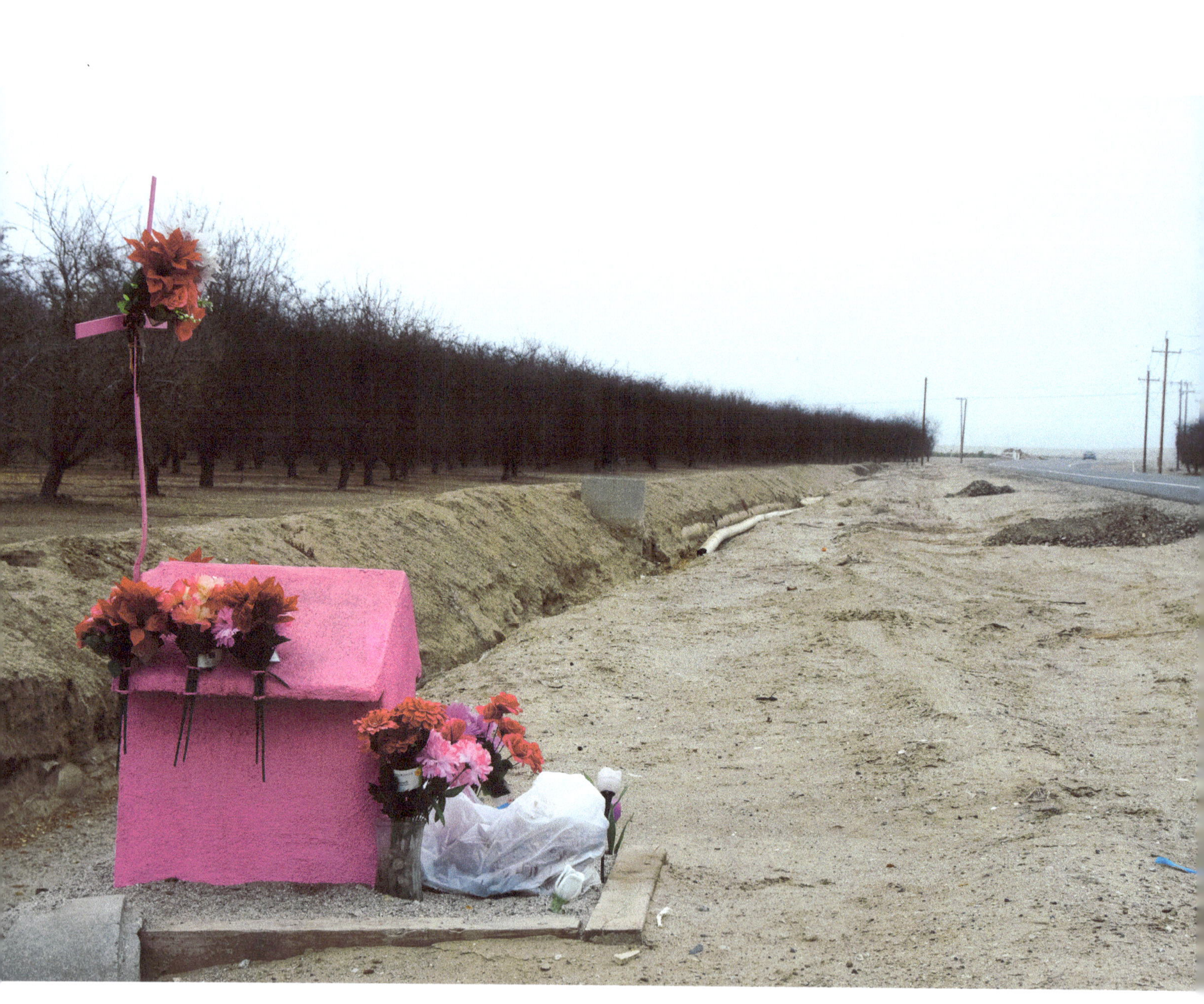

Donde Estas Papa?

Donde estas papa?
Where did you go?
I hardly knew you
I sat on your lap, held your hand
You plucked the spiky cholla from my tiny feet
Remember?

Donde estas papa?
I know you would not abandon me, forget me

Plastic orange and pink flowers
They are my favorite
Like the ones in my room
From the San Luis summer festival

Donde estas papa?

We were on our way to get corn
To feed the javelina in the wash
The doves flew above us as we drove away

Down the winding road, so much dust papa
So much dust, I cannot see you
So much dust, so much dust
Papa?

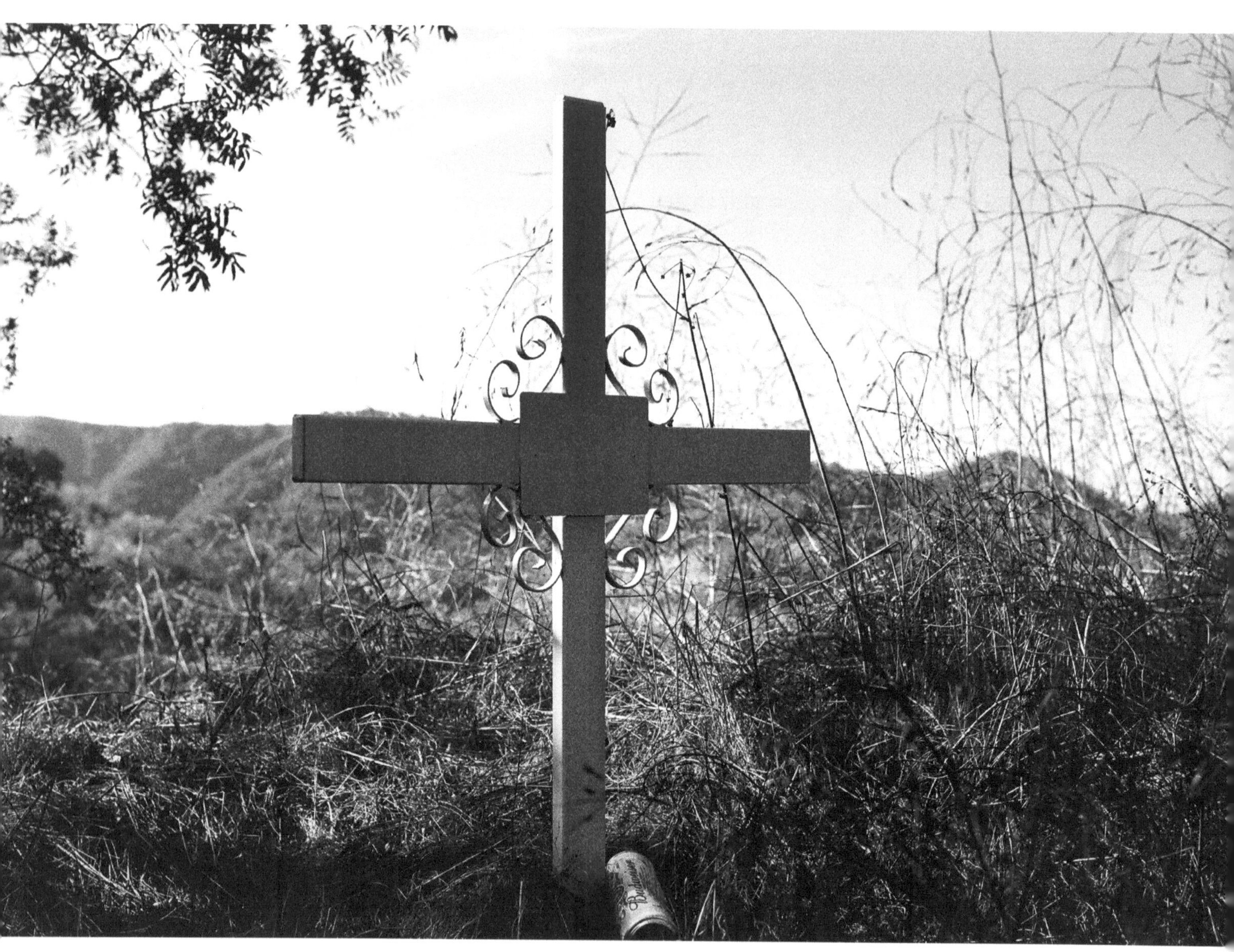

Topanga Cross, Topanga, CA 2010

Chicken Soup For The Soul

Jesus, all you guys do is stand around me
Going, "What he do that for?
That's dumber than shit!
Passin' a car and playin' chicken with a semi.
He was one crazy fucker!"

What the hell you guys come here for anyway?
You're just as crazy!

Why'd ya even put this stinkin cross here?
Don't cha know?

I'm Jewish

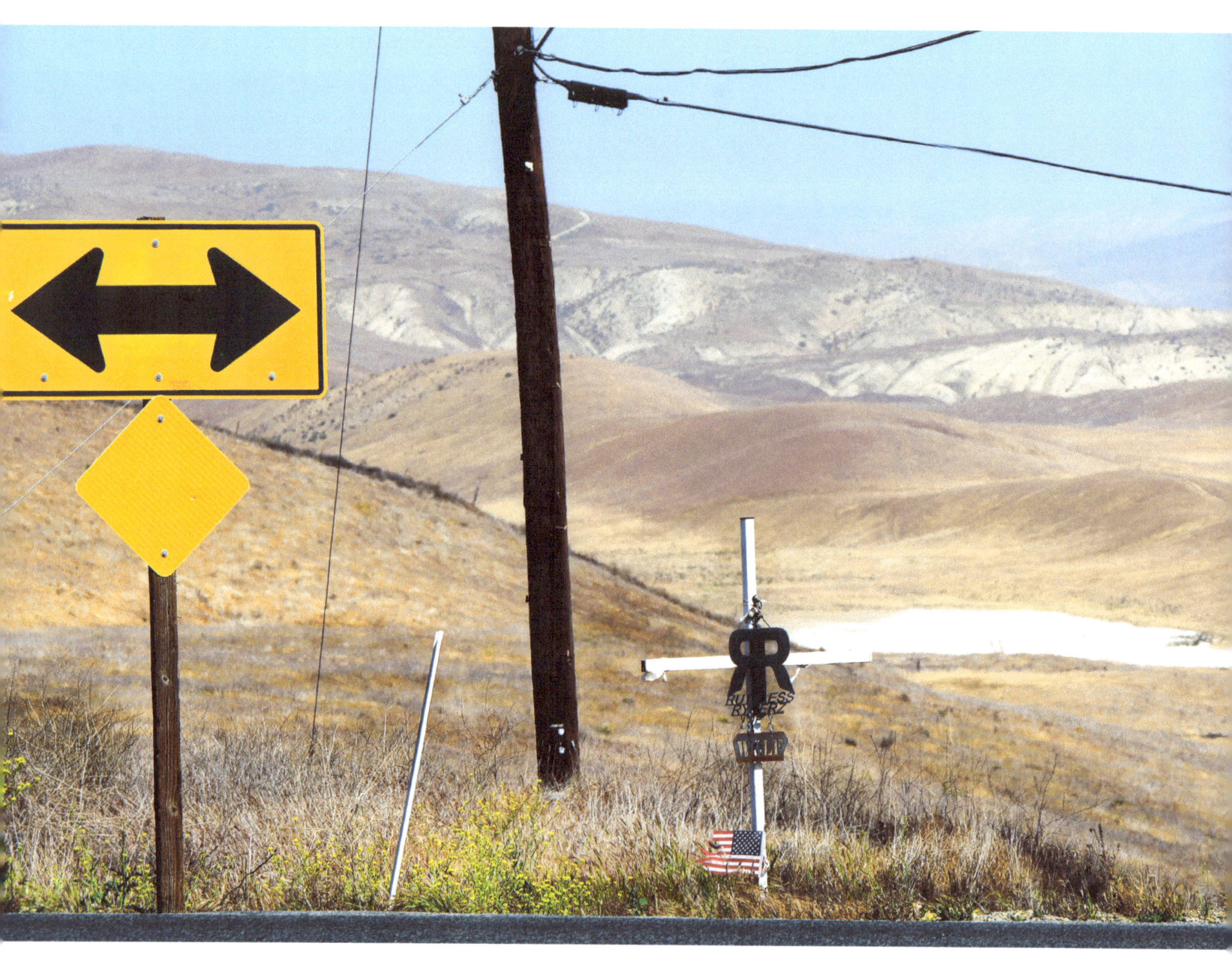

Wolf, Ruthless Ryderz, Santa Margarita, CA 2018

Fast

Fast, I wanted to go

Fast

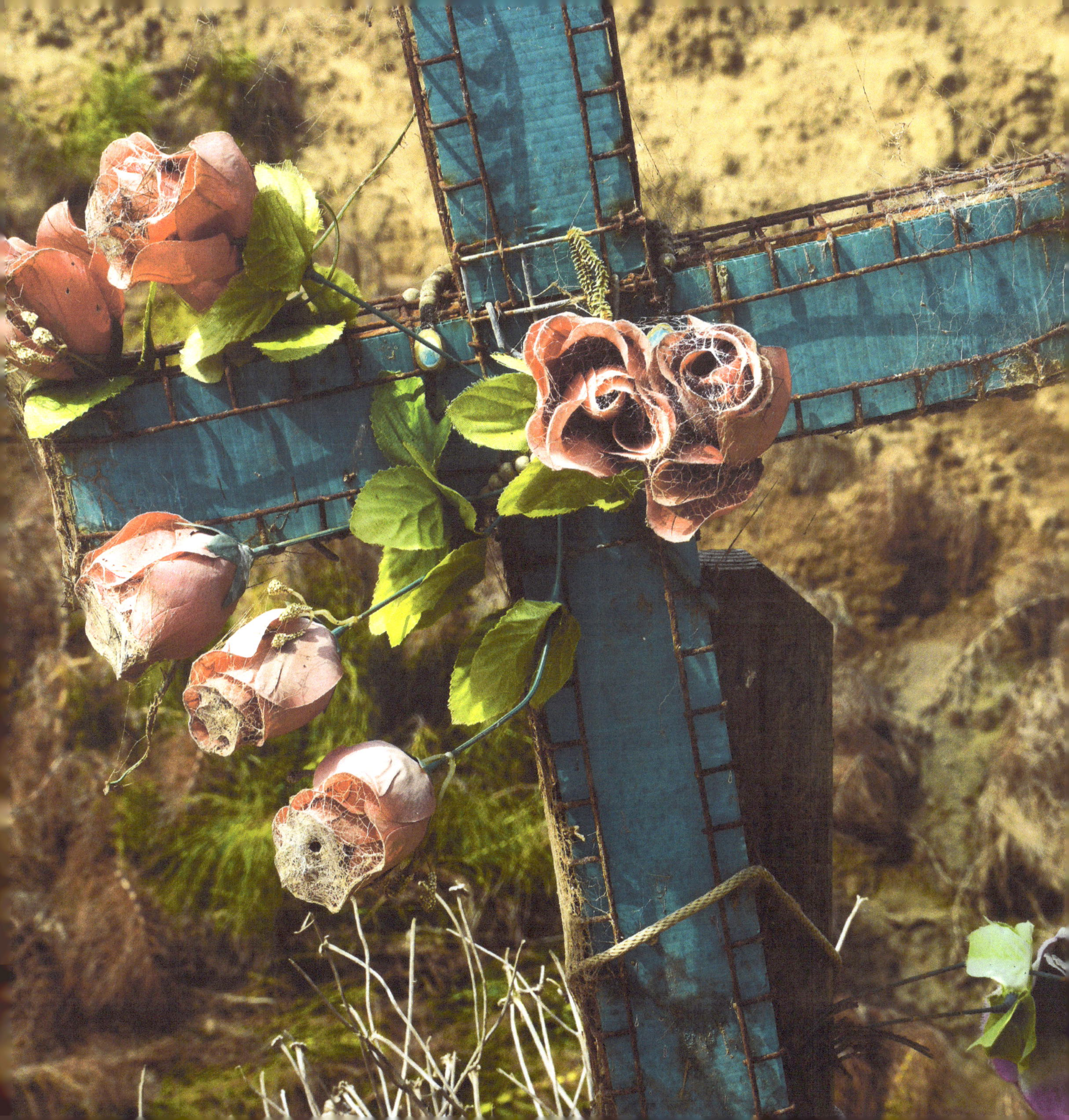

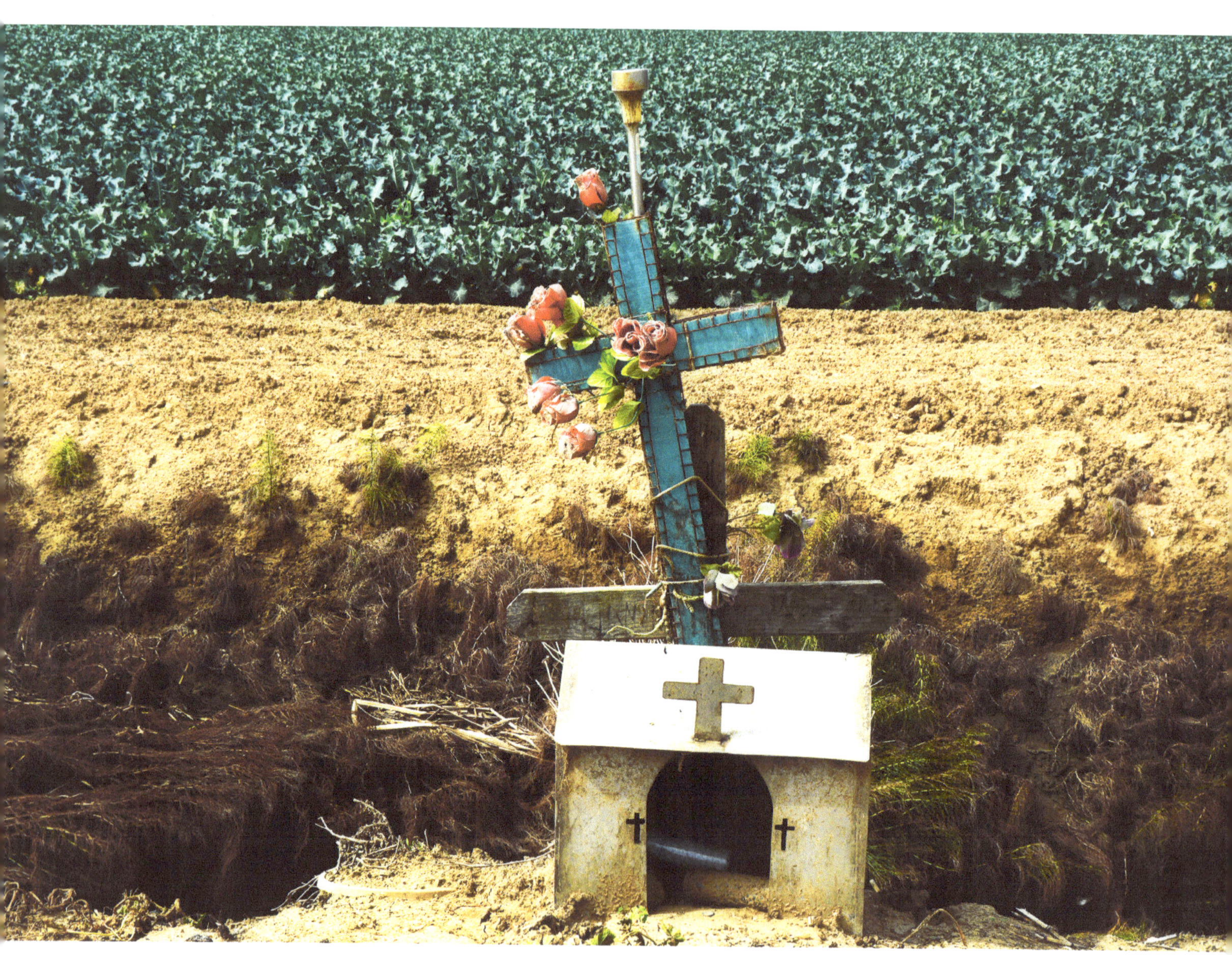

Guadalupe, CA 2015

Real Tulips

Hay, mi amor, today is Easter
I bring you tulips, real tulips

They won't last but the kids didn't want to leave plastic flowers today
So they picked out red tulips, real tulips

Y claro, they did not come with me, they are busy
Busy coloring eggs, azul, verde, roja, like the real tulips

They paint rainbows, cacti and like last year
They will paint your name, Victor, on one egg - in your memory

Ay, Victor, Victor, What else can I tell you?
My mother is still helping around the house
But her hearing is not so good

We all have to shout even louder than usual
That was a joke Victor, mi amor, I hope you are smiling

Hay, it's so windy today, my scarf is blowing off my head
Okay, Victor, I have to go home now and roast the pork
No one carves the pork like you, not like my Victor

Victor, Victor, the kids will come here manana to see you
And the tulips, the real tulips, Vaya con Dios,Victor

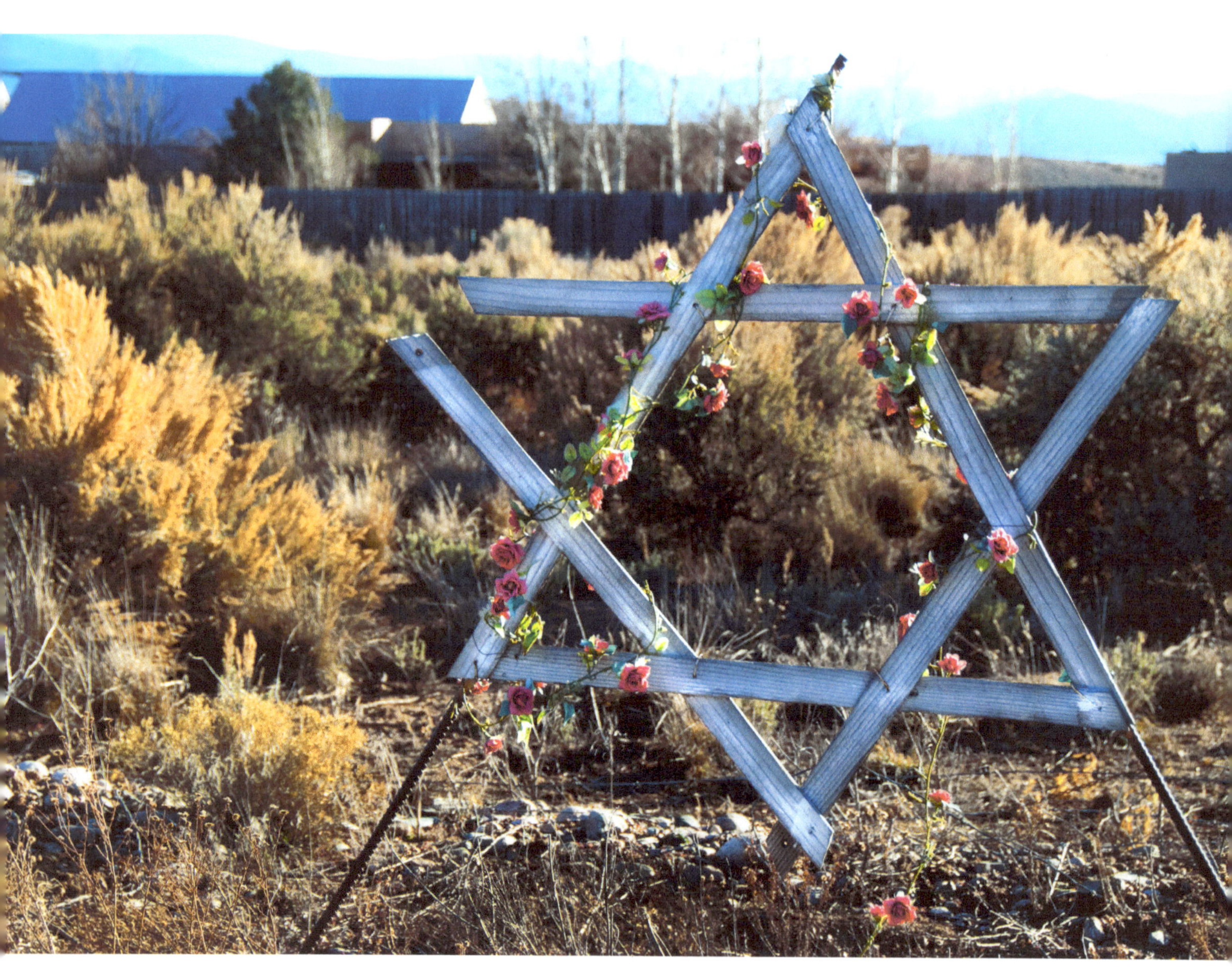

Star of David, Taos, NM 2011

Straight, No Chaser

I never knew what hit me
Like a shooting star
You came out of nowhere

You and me, on the same path
Traveling in the same direction

I was always a little ahead of you

You trailed me for a long time
Until I ran out of gas

You caught up to me

We collided

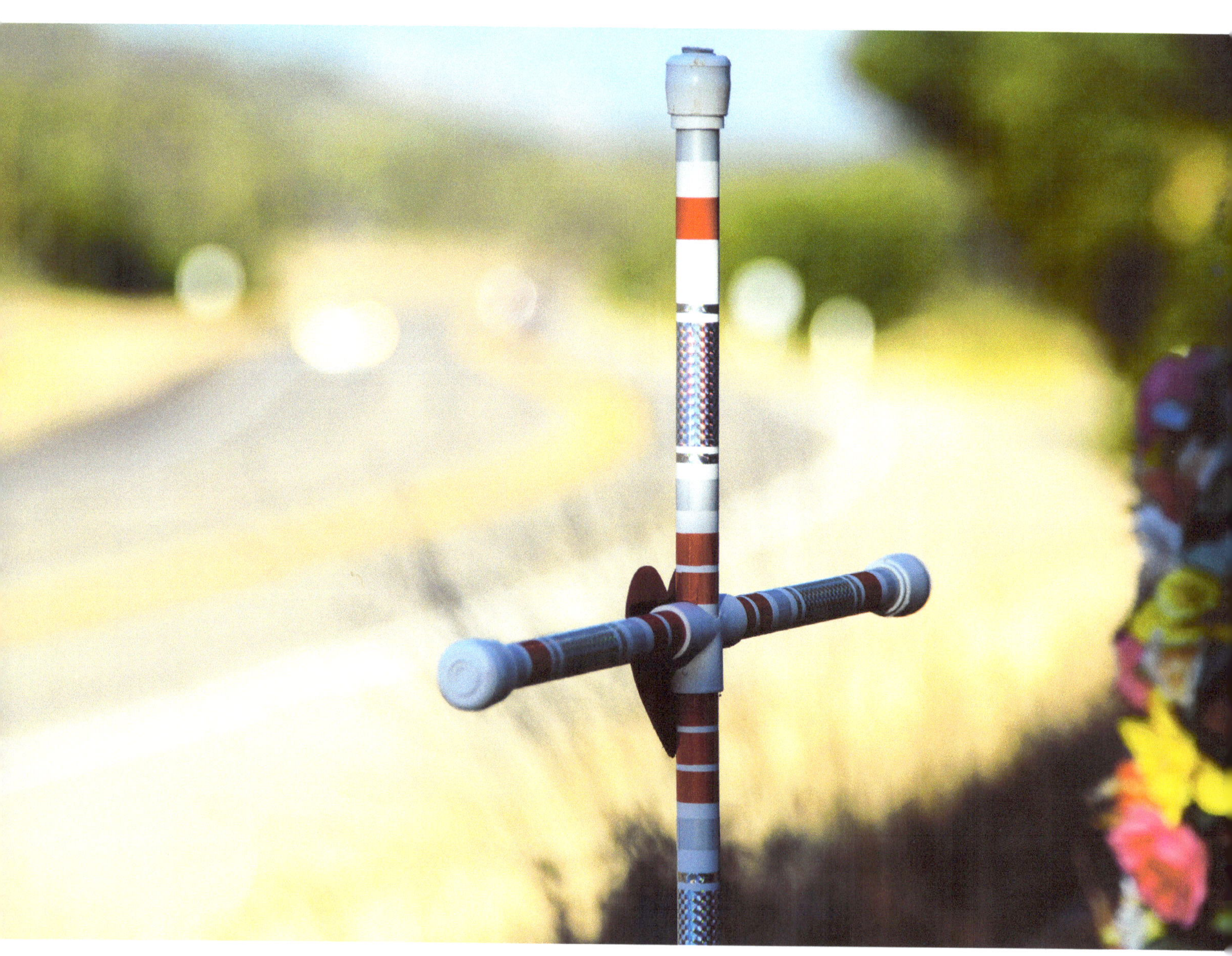

San Marcos Pass, HWY 154, CA 2015

Gold Medal

The torch is lit
Events have taken place
You place a wreath around my cross
I wear it like an Olympian

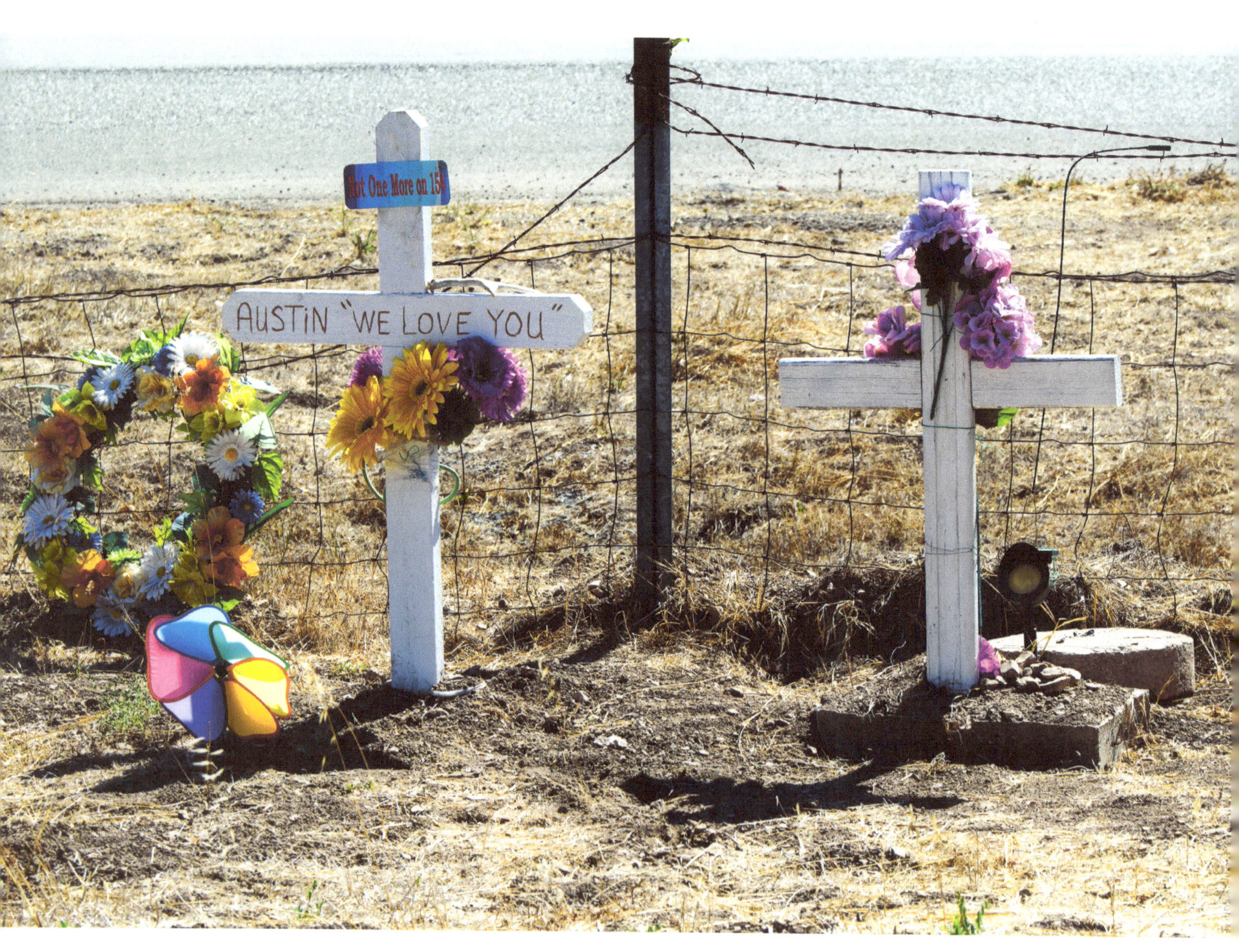

Not One More, Hwy 154, Los Olivos, CA 2017

I Don’t Speak For The Dead

I don’t speak for the dead
I only offer what I imagine

A voice
As if it were me
Killed on the journey
The Road

Amazed
That I am still alive
As I write this
While I drive

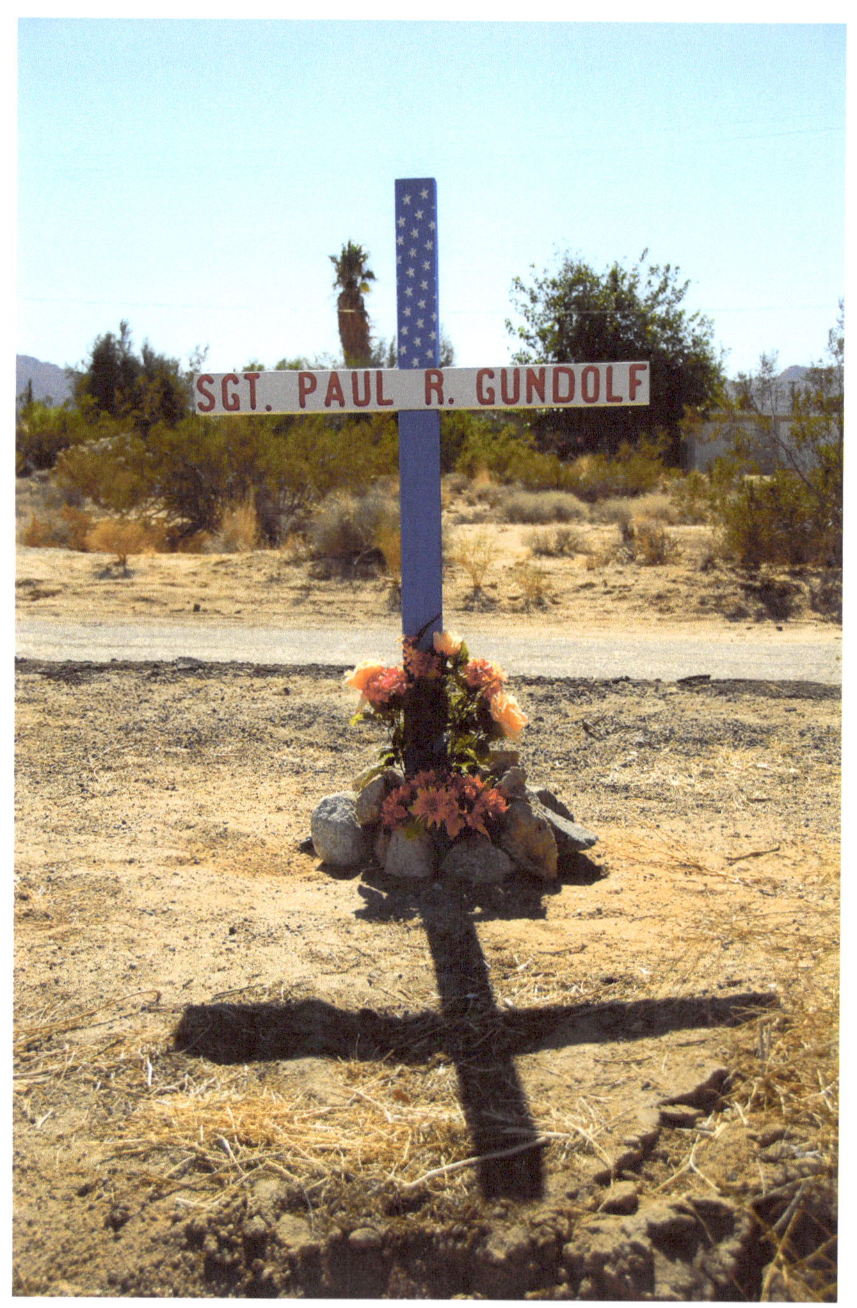

Sgt. Gundolf, Warner Springs, CA 2006

Red, White and…

The stark white cross
Symbol of death and memory

Rises from the crimson earth
Colors of perpetual sunset

There, in the red dirt
A ponderosa sapling
Young and green
Alive

In the background
Taps rings out its mournful melody
Of finality, anticipating the end of each note

The last inhalation
Followed by the tone
Until the breath

Runs

Out

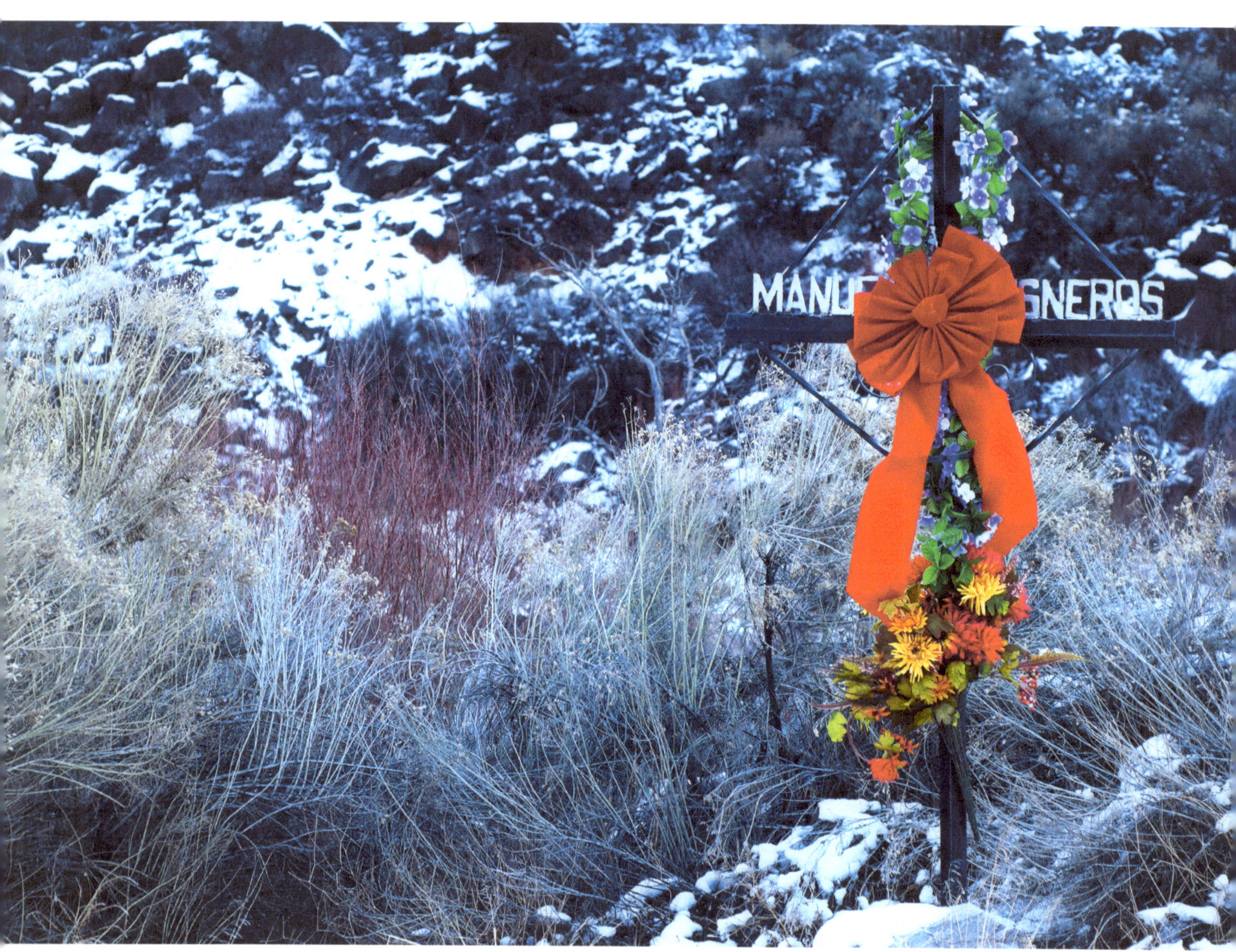

Manuel, Taos, NM 2011

One Snowy Night

You can barely see my cross in the snow
I'm not cold

Ah, the snow…that night
Lit by the rays of my headlights

Harmlessly, flakes fell like glitter
Innocently, kissing the ground before me

The ice lay like the devil in waiting
I am lost in the blizzard of eternity

Spinning, spinning, spinning
Into the white oblivion

A nocturnal traveler is blinded
Me or them?

The impact of one another…
Unforseen

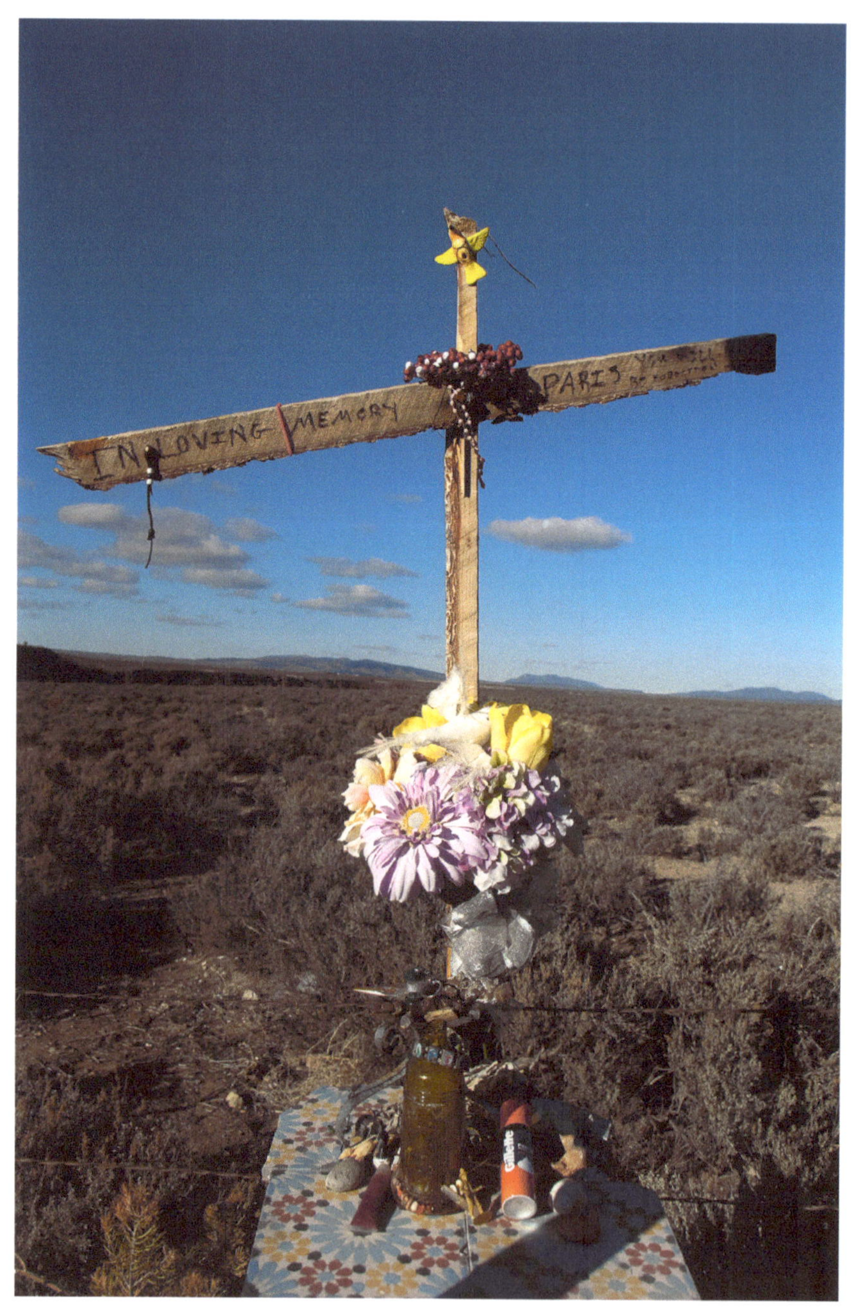

Paris, Taos, NM 2011

Eternal Spring

Crocus peeking through the ground
There are two
One yellow
One purple
Side by side
Entering Spring
Growing together
Stretching their petals
Igniting with rays of the sun
The rain falls
Nourishes their roots
Like ours, my husband and mine
Our souls lay
Beneath the ground
The earth we fertilized
Our blood, transfused

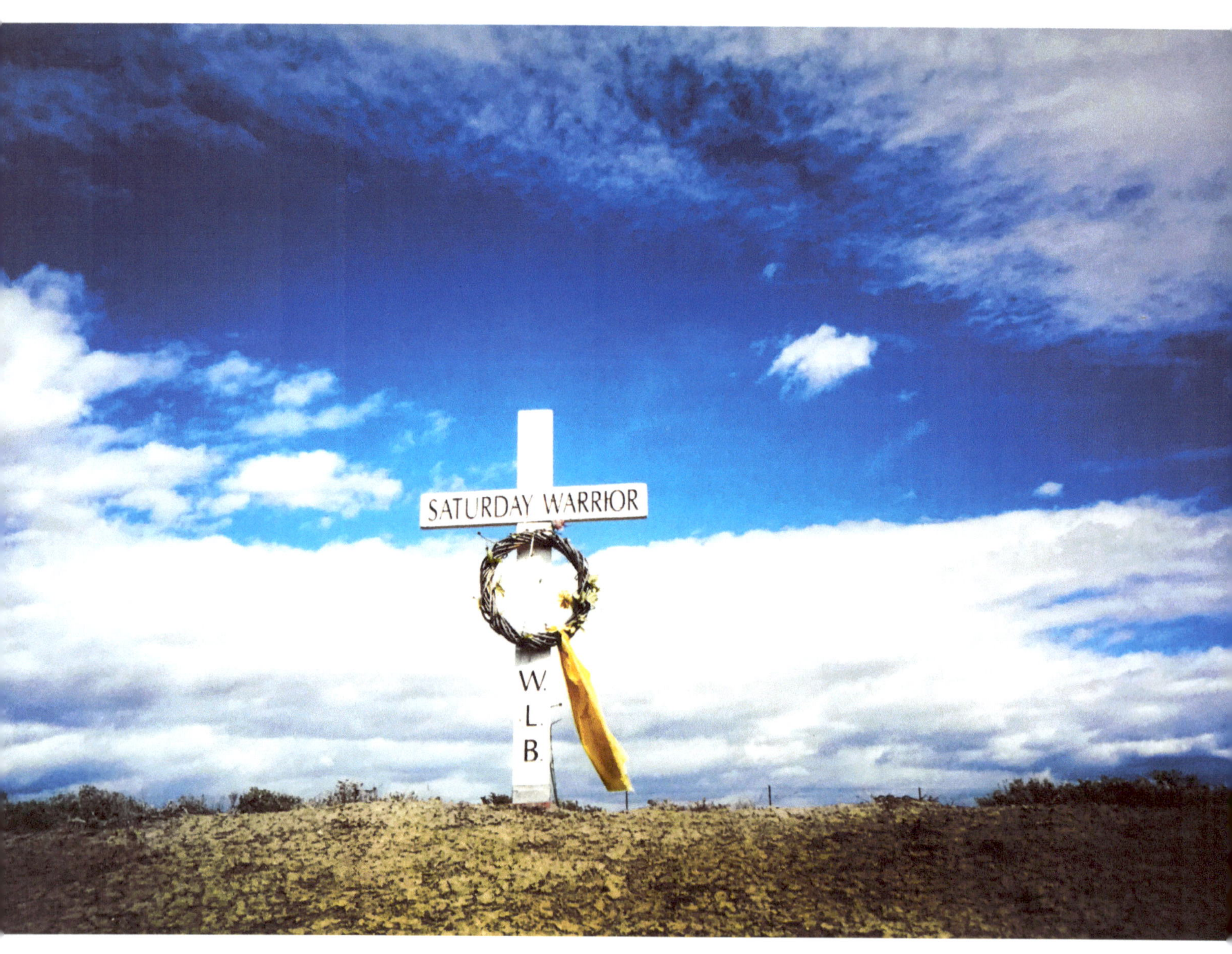

Saturday Warrior, Utah 2001

18 (Life) Wheeler

Oh, my cargo
My precious cargo
I transport you from state to state
How in the world could I lose you in Nebraska?
Such a flat road, a light load
My precious cargo
My precious cargo

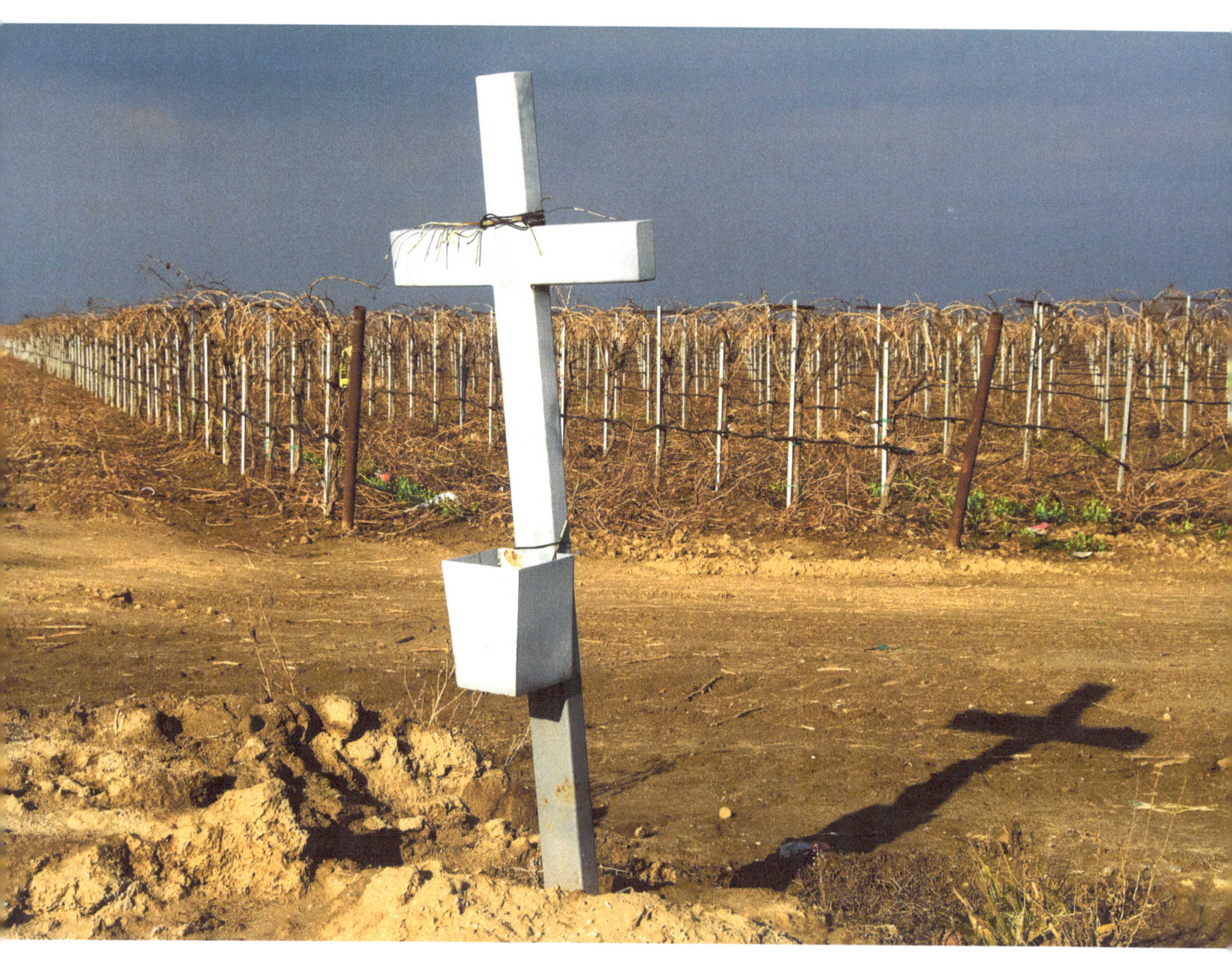

Bakersfield, CA 2018

The Grateful Dead?

Look at the tribute to my life
You can see many people loved me
Then and now

You shower me with flowers
Stuffed animals
Pictures

You stand over me
First sad with grief
Then smiling

You are glad the I am surrounded by such love
Such adoration
Do you want to trade places?

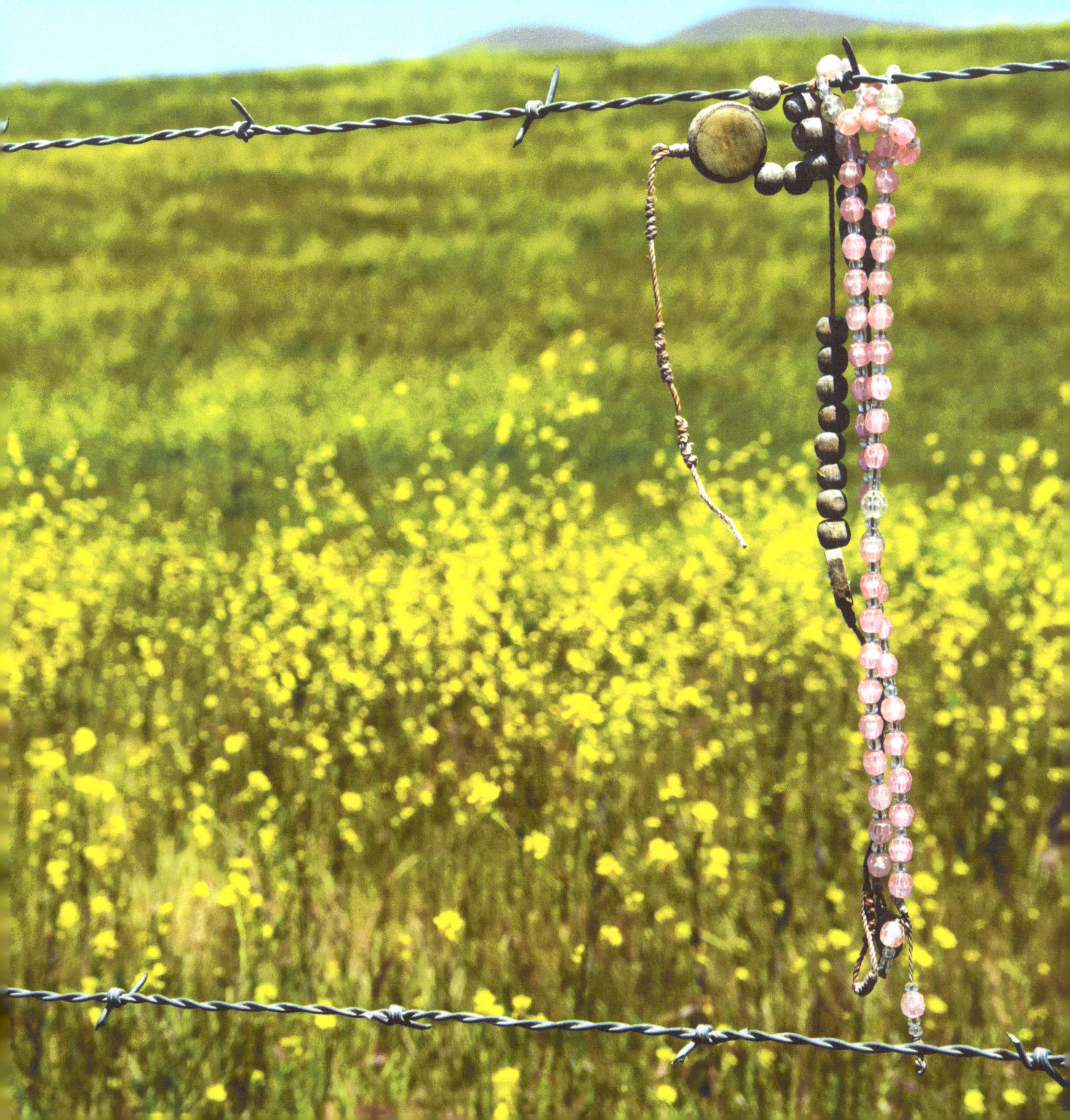

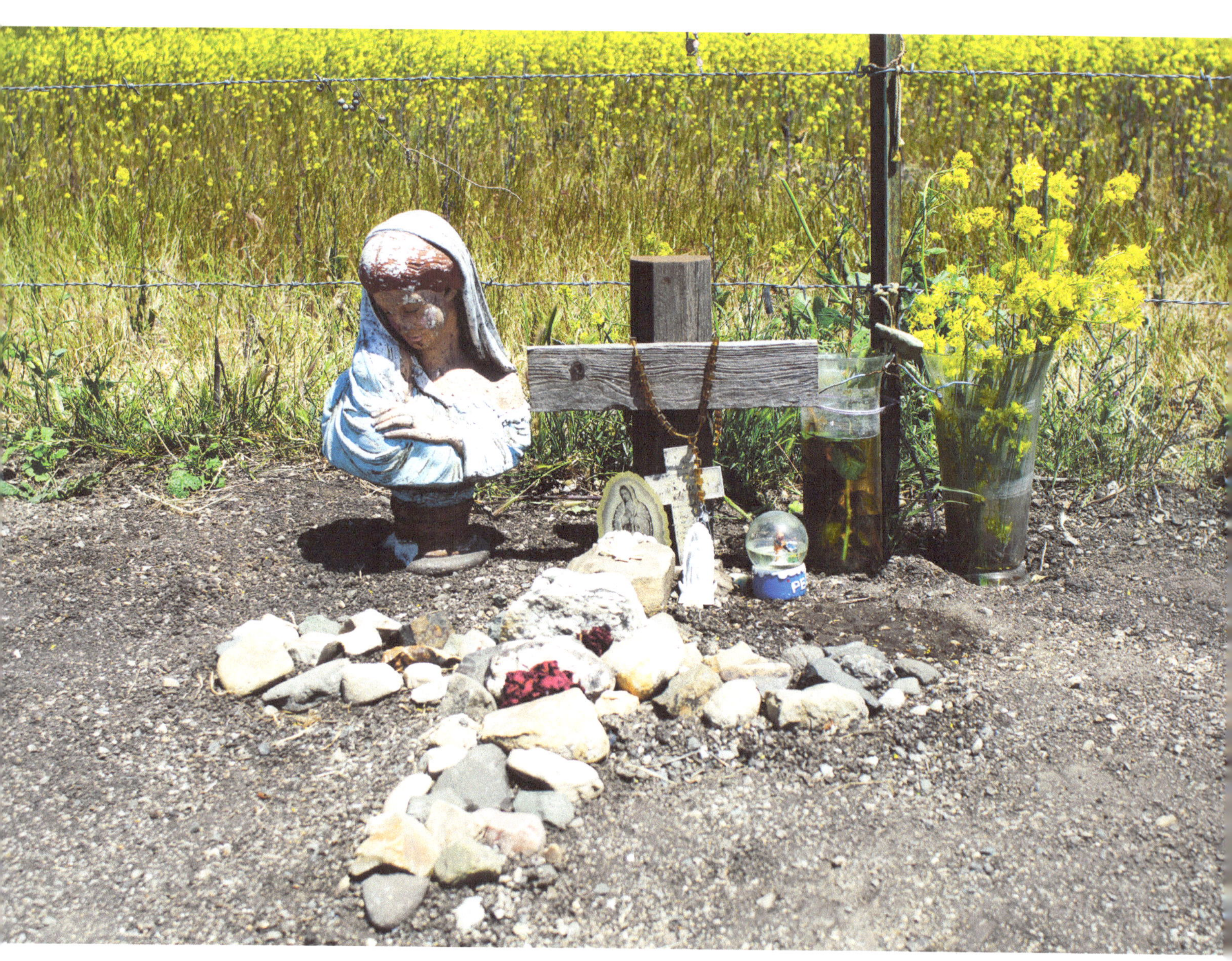

Yellow Fields, Santa Maria, CA 2018

Las Cruces

How many souls do we pass
On the sides of the highway?

Perched like crows on bleachers
As the parade of the living drives by

To ignore Las Cruces is to turn away from one's own soul
On this unpredictable road

We could be taken tomorrow
By nature, man, speed, recklessness, fate

Las Cruces
A journey to their destination

Some have barely been in the world
Others have been here twice as long as me
Three times as long as you
They leave stories, sadness, imagination and hope

Las cruces, reminders to stay awake
For those who live
For those who die
Las Cruces

Acknowledgments

I am extremely grateful to all who contributed to the publishing of this book and all who continue to contribute love and inspiration.

Joan Maiers, 18 years ago, you inspired me to write from my heart and soul. Thank you for editing the poetry in this book over 15 years ago and for composing such an eloquent and poignant foreword.

A millions thanks to Paula Mould, *The Book Closer*, for her guidance and expertise in self-publishing.

My comrades who give me objective feedback and continue to support me in so many ways: Rita Ross, Leigh Shenton, Suzanne Shelley, Abi Hodes, Corby Fleming, John Bennett, J. Michael Thompson, Salley Knight, Lisa Cox, Jeanne Glover, Theo Stephan and Deb Davis.

My beloved family and officemates (in spirit and in the now):
Luna, Nico, Shea and Joey.

As always, I am grateful for the love, patience and support of my favorite traveling companion and husband, Dave Salter, who never contests my request to hurriedly pull over on the side of a road or dangerous highway so I can take a photograph. Thank you for sharing this life long road trip, I love you.

Las Cruces
(Intersections)

First Edition: October 2018
Printed in the United States

www.robbiekaye.com
robbie@robbiekaye.com

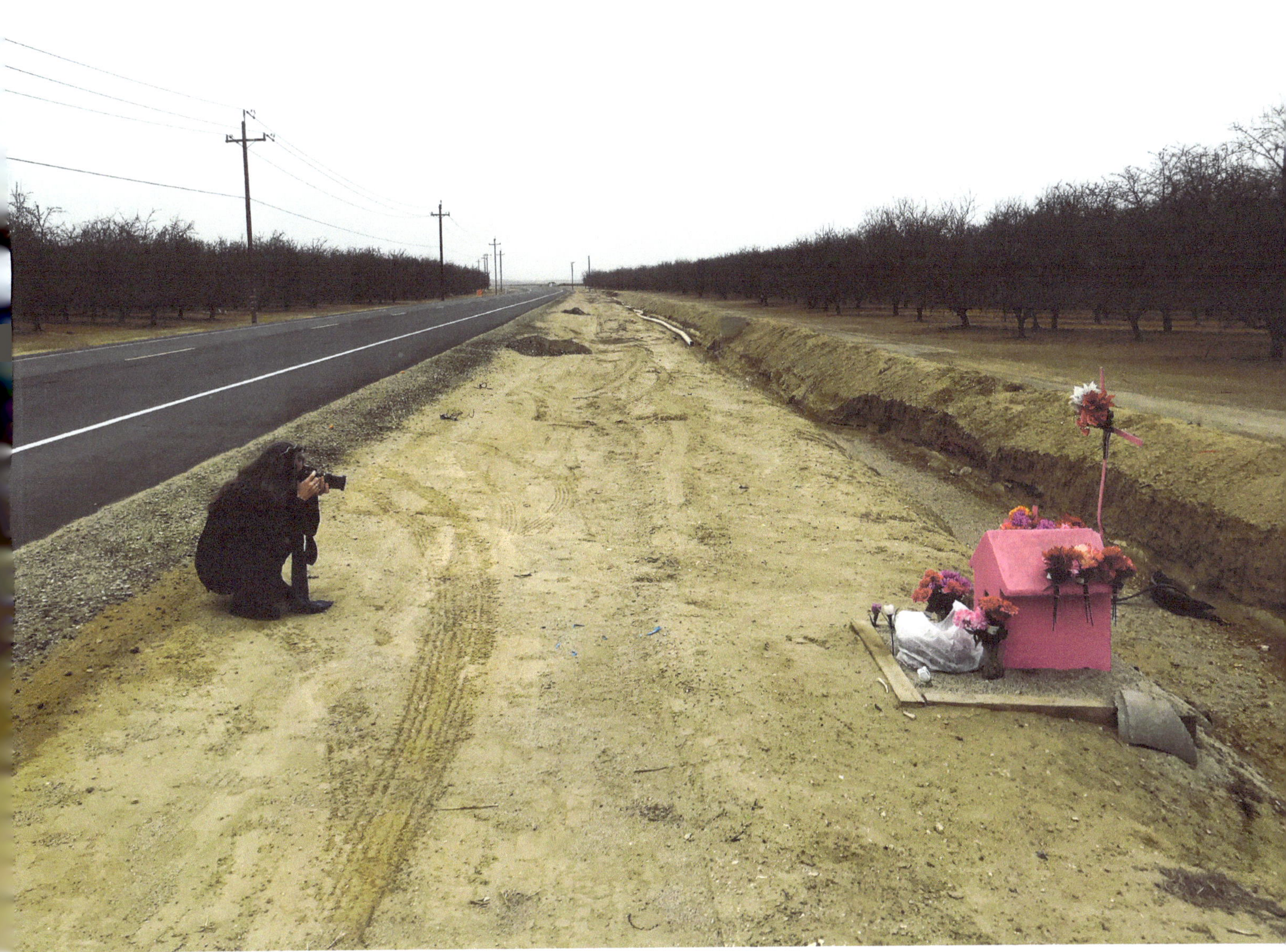

Photo: Dave Salter

www.ingramcontent.com/pod-product-compliance
Lightning Source LLC
LaVergne TN
LVHW070147110826
845147LV00002B/341

* 9 7 8 0 5 7 8 4 3 5 0 3 9 *